GEE'OR RUWERIN

GROWING UP IN SIXTIES PARSON CROSS

Steve Bush

ACM Retro
Published by ACM Retro Ltd,
The Grange,
Church Street,
Dronfield,
Sheffield S18 1QB.

Visit ACM Retro at:

www.acmretro.com
Published by ACM Retro 2011.

Steve Bush asserts the moral right to be identified as the author of this work.

A catalogue record for this book is available from the British Library.

GEE'OR RUWERIN
GROWING UP IN SIXTIES PARSON CROSS

Family Christmas dinner 1964

Gee'or Ruwerin

Parson Cross view

Contents

To MPB - an April Fool is for life,
not just for Grand National Day.

Gee'or Ruwerin

Chapter One

T'second house passed t' garage

I remember being born.

Well that's not exactly true. I don't really remember it, but I've heard the story of it so many times, it seems as though I was there!

Okay, so technically I was there, but I guess you know what I mean…

By all accounts I was an awkward sod from day one. Head first? Not for me. I chose to come out bum first, nearly killing my mum. Literally. I was the seventh of eight kids, and because the preceding bunch were typical young children, my mum decided on a home birth, allowing her to look after them right up until the chosen time. Luckily there was a very capable midwife on hand, and I was eventually delivered safely. Healthy, if slightly battered.

Legend has it that my dad had been suspicious of my parentage, but when I finally arrived I looked so like him that there was no way he could disown me.

My sister and brothers were all a bit disappointed when they found out. Not because they wanted a girl, or even a puppy, but because it meant that the meagre weekly spice allowance would now have to stretch that little bit more. Four fingers of Kit-Kat don't divide into seven mouths very well.

My birth coincided with the end of rationing, which was just as well, as I was always starving.

My family lived on the Parson Cross (woebetide anyone who calls it Parson's Cross), in t'second house passed t' garage. Although at that time, there was no garage. It was a field, and it rung to the joys of children playing right up until 1960, when Cleveland opened their filling station.

Here is my story as I remember it.

The epi-centre of Parson Cross in its infancy – Wordsworth Avenue and Deerlands Avenue junction with the Parson Cross Hotel in the background

Chapter Two

"I've brock mi tooer!"

I guess that my very first actual memory, the first one I can really grab a hold of, was of something that happened a few weeks after my third birthday.

It was a warm summer day, and I was out playing in the back garden. Mum was well into her eighth pregnancy and had plenty to do, cooking and cleaning for the six surviving offspring. Apart from an occasional glance through the kitchen window, and me popping back in for drinks of water, (the kitchen floor was knee deep in suds, and the mangle was working overtime, so the kitchen was not a good place to be!) I was left pretty much to my own devices.

It was a nice garden. A flat central lawn surrounded by flower beds and a couple of laburnum trees. At the top end was a greenhouse, but that was out of bounds in those days, the latest crop of tomatoes and cucumbers being close to fruition …

Mum and Dad had moved up to The Cross in the late forties. They'd met during the war. Mum was a nurse who came across from Ireland, along with thousands of her fellow country girls, to help with Britain's war effort. Dad came from a family of movers, and so had no natural home town. He served with the Royal Artillery, and met up with mum while receiving medical treatment.

Their first home in Sheffield was a "house share" on Albert Rd. Living in two rooms with common facilities, they managed to bring three kids into the world, two of them before the war was over, and were expecting a fourth when they were allocated a house on the newly built Parson Cross.

Parson Cross was a large sprawling housing estate on the north side of Sheffield. Consisting of some ten thousand houses, and started just before the war, it was based on an area of farmland between Herries and Ecclesfield. For the original inhabitants, all of whom came from inner city estates such as Heeley, Attercliffe, Darnall and Hillsborough, it was an oasis. The designers provided lots of open spaces for kids to play in. There were fields, parks and easy access to the woods at Ecclesfield and Greno. On top of that each house had a garden front and back – a luxury in those post-war days of rations and allotments.

Mum wept when they picked up their key from the housing office, not sure what they were moving to but glad to be moving at all, and wept again when they got off the 49 at Margetson Crescent, walked up Wordsworth, and let themselves into number 387.

It was a beautiful house, built of startling bright new red brick, with pebble dash covering the larger surface areas, and having a deep red tiled roof. Second in a group of four, it had an indoor bathroom and toilet, large front room, three good size bedrooms, and was very close to fields, which the older kids started exploring immediately. The kitchen was probably the weak link. It was a funny "L" shape, and didn't lend itself to being used as a diner, but it was certainly functional, and at the time one was very thankful for those small mercies. Compared to the old estate, which had suffered from being fifty years in the shadow of the factories and draped

Gee'or Ruwerin

in all the grime that they produced, it just seemed to be a marvel of red brick and green foliage, clear roads and open spaces, an urban utopia in which to raise a large family.

The three houses sharing our block became occupied during the same few days, and the four married couples, of similar age and station, would be friends and neighbours for the next twenty years. (Mum eventually left the house for sheltered accommodation fifty years to the day after she moved in).

In the garden I had a few simple toys – I seem to remember a set of wooden soldiers which I'd arranged in football team formation – and a bowl of soapy water, but my attention was focussed on a small blackboard, perched on an easel under the kitchen window. For some reason, now lost in the mists of time, I wanted to move it to the top end of the garden, and instead of shouting for help – much good that would have done on washday – I figured that I could carry it there myself. Now, a thing to bear in mind is that this wasn't the modern, light, convenient chalkboard that you can pick up from Early Learning these days. This was an iron board which was about a half inch thick, and weighed roughly the same as a small car. One surface was covered in a kind of black pitch and used for chalking, the other was a sort of green corrugated rust. I had moved everything else to my new favourite spot, beside the greenhouse. It was just a case now of moving the board, so I formulated a plan. Stretching my arms in a kind of star formation, I tilted my head, and took hold of it, top and bottom, at opposite corners. Having got a good grip of it, I leaned back and lifted, taking the brunt of the weight on my puffed out chest. So far, so good. It felt comfortable so I moved to stage two, turning my body in the direction of the lawn and slowly edging forwards in small careful steps. I walked and breathed in time, and stopped every few feet to recover. At the lawn edge there was a small concrete slab forming a path, and as I stepped onto it, my foot caught the lip, causing me to stumble forward and drop the board, corner first, on to my right big toe. To this day I can feel the pain shooting up my leg and bursting through my body. I tried to cry and scream at the same time, but although my open mouth was moving, trembling, no sound came for about five seconds. When it did however, it took the form of a loud blood-curdling scream. I ran limping around the garden shouting "I've brock mi tooer! I've –sob – brock – sob, mi too-oo—err!" Mum recalled years later how, on hearing the scream, she stopped mangling and looked out of the window, to see me hopping, jumping and leaping around the garden, yelping at the top of my voice. I alternately picked up my foot, and put it down again. I ran clockwise, then anti-clockwise, round the laburnum tree. I even ran to the top of the garden, twice around the green washpole, then back down again, and despite my obvious pain, my antics made her laugh. She stood back until I had stopped running and was now sobbing quietly, before coming out and giving me the TLC I so richly deserved. She bathed my foot, topping up the soapy play water with some from the kettle, with me going "ow, OW!!" every few seconds. My throbbing toe was then wrapped in the biggest bandage you ever saw, making it look like something from The Beano, (you could see it throbbing through the bandage!!) and I was led inside, carefully avoiding the washday suds, and I laid on the couch just in time to watch Andy Pandy and Teddy. A blanket from upstairs appeared and completed my comfort, and I must have dosed off, as the next thing I remember I was being woken up with scrambled egg on toast (still a favourite) and a cup of sweet tea.

I never saw the blackboard again.

Chapter Three

"Wot's Appleyards dooin in aar field?"

"Eh up Mrs, what's tha reckon to this then?"

My mum was hanging out the washing as I scooted around the garden, banging into her about once every three laps. My toe was well on the way to healing now, and only hurt when mum needed help carrying the washing.

She looked across at Mr Booker next door, (we pronounced it Booo-ker rather than Bucker) then over his shoulder on to the field where he was pointing. Three large purple trucks had pulled onto the field where Ian Booker and me normally rode his bike, and were circling around like Indians. They were followed by a yellow bull-dozer, a small dumper truck, and some official looking vans.

"Good heavens. What do you think is happening?" Her Irish brogue had softened over the years to a kind of neutral accent, but she had resisted picking up the 'thees and thas' her children employed.

"Looks like thi building summat" He replied.

In retrospect, it was inevitable that the fields of my childhood would eventually become building sites, but it was still a shock when it started happening.

"Stephen, come back here!!!"

I was off down the entry on my scooter, and well on the way to investigating this mystery by the time I didn't hear her. I turned into the field, scooted along the dusty path, and pulled up sharp when a man with a clipboard blocked my way.

"Wot yer dooin' on aar field?"

Clipboard man looked at me with barely disguised disdain.

"Bugger off or al githee a clip rarn't lugoil"

The pencil behind his ear twitched.

Ignoring him, I spun back on to the pavement, went a further few yards along and turned back onto the field, this time hiding behind a truck, and watched.

Three men were gathered around a tripod mounted with a small telescope, and looked through the eyepiece at another guy who was holding up a big blue and white ruler with one hand. From his other, hung a piece of string with a whipping top at the end. He moved around the field, stopping every few yards, and the telescope team followed him with the instrument. Clipboard man wrote all this down.

After about half-an-hour, one of the truck's sides was lowered down and a man with a cap on started throwing picks and shovels off. His team-mates picked them up and, reluctantly at first, began digging.

I tried talking to them but they didn't answer, so after a handful of attempts, I pushed my scooter back home.

"What's happening on the field?"

"Some mesters are dooin' some diggin' and some others are tekkin pictures wi' a telescope, an a man wi a booerd threatened to gi' me a clip!!" I followed this with an explosion of breath.

Mum just nodded, as if it all made sense, and went back to pegging white shirts on to the line.

A few hours later the twins came home from school. Although very different, they often said the same thing at the same time.

"Mam, Wot's Appleyards dooin in aar field?"

There were now more trucks, and the digger was starting to turn over huge clods of earth, and pile them up neatly on the path we used for access. The twins walked over to the edge of the field, with me scooting along behind them, and joined the other kids in watching their playground get turfed over.

"Nah then Bushy, as tha seen this?" Dave Baldwin, using the universal Bush family nickname, watched eagle eyed as a small dumper started piling bricks up on the first available piece of flat ground.

"Wot thi buildin'?"

"Ant gorra clue. One er 'em sez it's a pub an't other reckerns it's gunna be a new Skoyl"

"A Skoyl??" there was a chorus of dismay at this.

"Wot do we need a Skoyl for? Wiv got loads as it is."

Saddened at the prospect of a new school on their doorsteps, the kids drifted off home in ones and twos, and not long afterwards, the builders did too.

"Thiz a piece abaht it in t'final- it in't gunna be a Skoyl, its gunna be a gar-arge."

John was telling his friends later that day, as they stood on our back path gazing over the hedge at the deserted building machines. A garage – pronounced garridge – was a small stand alone building, usually next to a house or on a site with other garridges, where vehicles were kept overnight. But a garage – pronounced gar-arge – was a commercial premises, made up of some combination of filling station, vehicle repair centre, and maybe a shop. This was to be all three and would come with the bonus of living quarters above. That meant new neighbours, always a point of interest.

"Mi mam sez that Appleyards are building it for them senn's, an it's gunna be fam-ly run."

At that time Appleyards were striving for world domination, and looked like achieving it. Grown ups spoke a lot about fingers and pies where the Appleyards were concerned.

"Mind, It's gunna tek ovver a yea-er ter build."

John's mate Ray was firing a home made catapult at the big shovel on the digger, but his half-hearted efforts all fell short of their target, and having discussed it to death, they went off down t'Milnrow to play hiddy.

Gee'or Ruwerin

Chapter Four

"Weerz that teapot thing?"

"Mam! Weerz that teapot thing?"

"What teapot thing?"

Puzzled doesn't quite do it. Perplexed maybe.

"The teapot?"

"Nay-ew, that white teapot thing wi't lid wot Uncle Frank 'ad"

Puzzled pause...

"Oh, you mean his billy-can? I think it's in the cupboard"

She opened the pantry up and handed down a white enamelled jar, chipped blue in places, with a wired carrying handle, and the lid stored upside down on top, her puzzled look slowly becoming more intense

"Can yer dumee some tea innit?"

At this she stopped completely, and tried to fathom out why on earth her three-and-a-half year old son would suddenly want to start drinking his tea out of a builder's billy-can.

The previous year, Mum's younger brother Frank, had come across to England, and like many of his fellow Irishmen, had set out to make his fortune in the building trade. During his first few months, he'd used our house as a base while he got himself set up with work. Much of his initial work had been casual, so he would move about during the week, lodging in whatever digs were available, and coming back to ours at the weekend. It must have been a bit of an imposition for my parents, what with a large young family and all, but Frank was such a lovely guy that it never seemed like a problem. In fact, when he eventually moved out, and set himself up in business building tennis courts for rich people in Surrey, we all missed him terribly.....

......And he left his billy-can behind.

"What do you mean 'you just do'"??

"I just do!" Bit of frustrated foot-stomping

"That's not an answer. You can't just decide to drink your tea out of a billy-can Stephen. There must be a reason behind it."

"It's them mesters...."

A light bulb lit above her head as Mum's quizzed face slowly eased into one of enlightenment, and she went to the sink to fill the kettle.

Now that building was well underway on our new petrol station, I had taken it on myself to monitor progress, making sure that everything was done by the book, and to see that the brickies put the walls up properly. I'm not sure what the builders thought of their pre-school foreman, but they were all so nice to me that I rapidly became one of the team, or at least it felt like it.

Gee'or Ruwerin

Hence the billy-can.

I ran up the dirt path towards the hut, holding the billy-can in one hand, and a jam sandwich in the other.

"Would you look at that..." Not the same accent as mum's but very similar "The rascal's only gone and got himself a billy!" Their looks betrayed incredulity, as I climbed up on the bench beside them and plonked my "lunch" down on the wooden table.

"Where in the world did you dig that up from?" More Irish

"Mi Mam sez I can 'ave this nah that Uncle Frank's gone dahn south.." I lied "..so I can have mi dinner 'ere evry day nah"

I was quite sure that this would please them no-end, so I didn't need to look at their faces as they went on chewing their beef sandwiches, washing them down with Typhoo. I busily dug in to my jam sarny, and poured a measure of tea into the lid/cup, and sipped it gratefully, giving a loud "Aaahh" and smacking my lips after each mouthful. Boy was I dignified!!

During that year, my last before school, I spent a lot of time with those guys. There must have been moments when they just wished that I would go away, but if there were, they never let on. A couple of them, mostly the Irish guys, kept me informed of what they were doing, using in-house terms that I've long forgotten, and they even let me lay a few bricks, scooping up the gobbo with a small trowel, and carefully spreading it onto the existing line of bricks before placing a new line of bricks on top.

I constantly pestered them with dumb questions, but they always took the time to answer.

"What's that foh?"

"Now sure, that's a dumper truck."

"What's one o'them when it's at ooerm?"

My mum sometimes came and spoke to them, probably chatting about the old country, but always well out of my earshot. She would often boil a kettle up for them, especially when it got a bit colder and their primus stoves found it harder to do the job. She seemed to sense when I might start getting on the poor guys' nerves, and always called me in "Stephen - Rag Tag and Bobtail are on!" before it got tedious.

For years afterwards, I always felt that I'd played a part in building that Petrol Station, and was genuinely sad when, some twenty years later, they knocked it down and built a modern "franchised" contraption. It was a big part of my growing up, and had been many things to me.

It was a football pitch, the tarmac area at the rear providing a perfect playing surface, and the doors of the private garages ideal as goals.

It was an adventure park, climbing on garage roofs and jumping from one to the next, and then into a tree, being a terrific way of filling the school holidays

It was somewhere to buy fags (they're for mi mam – honest!) and somewhere to smoke them, there being lots of nooks and crannies round the back where adults would never venture.

Gee'or Ruwerin

It was also where, at the grand old age of five, I first fell in love

The first proprietors were relatives of the Applyards (I think), and they had a daughter my age called Janet.

Janet was everything a five year old boy could want in a girlfriend. She was pretty, she was clever, and best of all, she swore! (Not proper adult swearing, just bums and buggers, and definitely not when grown-ups were listening, only when we were out playing on the field.)

Up until then, I wasn't even aware that girls could swear, never mind that they would. I was fascinated and spent hours thinking of words that I could dare her to say (she always did, but with an air of contrition, which somehow made it better).

I even taught her a few Irish ones that I'd picked up from the builders ("Bejayzus" and the like), and her attempts to mimic my brogue, itself a mimic, were funny and delightful

Sadly Janet didn't stay round our way long. After a couple of years her family flitted, and the garage was taken over by their cousins (the two dads were brothers). I was heartbroken, and although the new family had a boy my age (another Stephen would you believe?) with whom I became good friends, it simply wasn't the same.

The new garage, which replaced the original after twenty odd years, wasn't built with anything like the same care and attention. It was all plastic and well lit and clean and didn't have oil spills and had assistants who wore smocks and all the horrible things that came with the 1980s, but I guess that's what rose-tinted specs can do for you.

(Back row - left to right): Paddy Bush, Michael Bush, Linda Senior, not known, Kath Bush, George Glaves (middle row) not known, Peter Bush, John Bush (front row) Brian Wigglesworth, Paul Neath, Dave Goodwin, Derek Glaves, Steven Senior, Steve Bush, Ian Booker and Pete Wrigglesworth.

Chapter Five

Three-one-oh-one-oh

"Stephen!"

"Wot?"

"Can you pop down down to The Stores and get me a pint of milk and some tea?"

"The Stores" was a generic name for the Co-Op, or to give it its full name, The Brightside and Carbrook Co-Operative Society.

Sheffield had three Co-Ops in those days: B&C, S&E (Sheffield and Ecclesall), and one more I can't remember. What I can remember though is that their name was quite oxymoronic, as they couldn't even co-operate with each other never mind anything else. If you shopped in a Co-Op outside your own area, then your divi was worthless. Imagine today a Tesco Clubcard which can only be used in a small number of geographically located shops. It was none the less a friendly place, where people knew each other by name, and the annual divi pay out helped Mum through the expense of Christmas each year.

"O-reight. Gi uz t'money."

We had just got out of the car after returning from a week's holiday in Brid.

A lovely week in a pink caravan, hiding from the rain and listening to Charlie Chester on the wireless. I love fish and chips but I think it's fair to say we overdosed on them that week, and the van smelled constantly of vinegar. I remember also the wind, coming in from the North Sea, rattling through the bunk I was sleeping in (I say 'bunk' – 'cupboard' would be kind) and keeping me awake at night.

The days are a blurred memory of the usual seaside things. Donkeys, sandcastles, acute sunburn, that type of thing. I don't think we had factor 20 in those days. We tended to use chip fat, olive oil, nivea, calamine lotion, and anything else mum found in the pantry on the day we left.

The Beagle on Knutton Crescent – still going to this day

Gee'or Ruwerin

We got back early because my dad liked to avoid the traffic. We set off just as most people were getting to bed after a night out and reached home well in time for the Jack Jackson show.

I picked up the half-crown, and belted off in the direction of Margo shops. As I reached Wriggo's house I stopped suddenly. Wriggo was in the front garden playing with a little black puppy.

"Ooze is that?"

"Mine."

"We-erve yer gorrit from?"

"Ahr Alan gorrit from somebody at work."

As Alan worked at Owlerton Dog Track, this was indeed interesting news.

"Is it a grey'ound?"

Anyone who knows anything at all about dogs would know that, not only was this little puppy not a greyhound, but that it was quite obviously a Heinz 57 mongrel of the highest order. I however knew nothing about dogs, and figured if it was Alan's dog, it must be a racer.

"Cooerse it in't."

"Worrizit then?"

"Mungrel."

"Azit gorra name?"

"Blackie."

And so I first met Blackie, the dog who would be the bane of my life for the next ten years. Every time I went up Wriggo's path to knock their door, I would be attacked by this flippin' monster and end up runnin' back up the street as far as the jennel.

"Are tha comin' aht? We can tek it forra walk on t'field."

"Inabit. Ah've juss gorra gutter margo for mi mam."

This said, I continued my record breaking sprint as far as the 49 bus stop, and turned left up towards the shops.

As I walked up to Margetson shops it was like greeting an old friend. Firstly there was a piece of spare land which would eventually become the library, then we had the Co-Op Butcher, or "Jack" as mum called him, then the Co-Op itself. (There was also a Co-Op Funeral Parlour, but I can't remember if they had a shop or just an office in those days.) Next came Hulleys Butchers, then Shaws Newsagent and Lomas's Chemist Shop. After that the memory plays a few tricks but I remember it as The Hardware Shop (Shentons?) Leech's (not sure what their fare was but I remember they sold Jubblies) and then the Chip'oil.

I sauntered into the Co-Op in much the same way as I would saunter into The Beagle years later.

"Can I 'ave a pint o' milk please, and some Indian Prince for mi mam?" I shouted as I unloaded the coin noisily onto the glass top counter. The assistant reached behind her and picked out the two chosen items.

"What's your share number?" she asked, ringing it through the till.

"Three-one-oh-one-oh."

"Oh hello – Have you had a nice holiday?"

Chapter Six

Gooin to t'Flicks

"Is your Bushy in?"

"Stephen! Wriggo's here."

"Tell 'im ah'm cummin, ah'm just finishin' mi porridge."

I looked up from the table to see, not just Wriggo, but Kenny and Senna walk into the front room.

"Erry up or wi'll be late."

Wriggo was always straight to the point.

"Mam, can I 'ave mi money?" blurted through the last mouthful

She counted out eightpence from her purse onto the telephone table

"Ahh Mam, yer said I could 'ave a bob!!"

What she'd actually said was "No, you can't have a shilling, you can have eight-pence" but who am I to split hairs?

She looked at me with one of those "What are we going to do with you" looks and picked up the two loose pennies and replaced 'em with a tanner. I snatched both tanners up, before she could change her mind - "Fanks mam!" – and headed out through the door still swallowing porridge, followed by my three best mates

We decided to walk down to the Ritz and save ourselves an extra penny to spend on spice. Entrance was sixpence. If we walked home too, that would be tuppence saved, meaning I had a full tanner to spend. Just call me "Roth Child" (I had no idea who "Roth Child" was, but his name was usually associated with great wealth).

Saturday morning cinema was the highlight of the week. Every week we would set off, along with loads of other kids, for a weekly dose of cartoons, films, and action packed serials, at the "Ritz" cinema on Wordsworth.

Corner of Mansell Crescent and Chaucer Road

Gee'or Ruwerin

This lovely Art-Deco (ish) building normally showed two films a week ('A' and 'B' features). On any given evening, the films were constantly played on loop, so you could come in half way through, and sit there until it played around to the same point, at which you left. Sounds daft now, but that's what happened. Most grown-ups would sensibly time there arrival to coincide with the start of the programme, 'B' feature first, then 'A', but as kids we just turned up whenever. If it was a good film, you could watch it one-and-a-half times.

Saturday mornings though, were adult free zones. The "Flicks" would be packed to the rafters with screaming kids ready for their weekly dose. The formats varied a little, but were usually something like:

A Warner Brothers cartoon.

A Public Information Film.

A comedy short (Three Stooges, Alfalfa, that kind of thing).

A short break (birthday dedications, yo-yo competitions).

A Children's Film Foundation flick (usually starring Michael Crawford, Sally Thomsett or a very young Keith Chegwin).

A final cartoon.

Then (Da-DaaaH!!) The Serial.

The Serial was very much a boy's thing. The most famous example was "Flash Gordon" but there were lots of others – Captain Video and Captain Marvel are two that spring.

The format was similar in each case. A futuristic sci-fi set up, with a mature hero (in his thirties?) and an immature sidekick (seemed about twelve but was probably 17), a glamorous leading lady who didn't get to say or do much, and of course, a baddie.

The baddie had to be an ugly alien (often with oriental features I recall) and plans to conquer the universe. The hero and his teenage companion would naturally try to prevent this, in seven 30 minute episodes, each of which had a real cliffhanger ending, just to make sure you came back next week.

"Bushy, As tha brung thi yoyo?"

"Ahr I 'ave. I've nicked ar John's – it's a luny 99."

I proudly displayed the black shiny yo-yo for all to see, and mimicked it moving majestically up and down at my command before dropping it and chasing it under a privet hedge.

"E'll kill thee if 'e finds art – I saw 'im a bit back artside Baldwins."

"OO worree wee, worree wee izsen?"

"Nayew, 'e wor talkin' to BeeBee an Barbra."

"Yor John likes lasses dunnee?" This from Senna, who spoke little but was profound when he did.

"Norraif 'e dunt."

He was also the local yo-yo champ, and his Black Lunar 99 was a prize possession. I was skating on thin ice, but figured that this skill must be in the genes, and that I therefore, would soon be a yo-yo master.

Gee'or Ruwerin

It isn't and I wasn't.

On the way down we constantly flicked small stones at each other, played "tiggy", fenced with imaginary swords, and generally acted out the most recent episode of Robin Hood/William Tell/Fireball XL5 (perm any one from three). To break the monotony of the long walk we walked up one side of Wordsworth Crescent and down the other. I was looking out for Sharon who lived on the Crescent, and who had recently left our school to go Southey, but I didn't see her.

As we got to the "Buggut" (Bug Hut) the doors were still closed ("Wriggo, I thought tha said wid be late??) and there was about four thousand kids (ok, 80 kids, but it seemed a lot more at the time) waiting to get in

"Eh up Bushy!!"

It was Richard from school. He lived on Launce Rd.

"Eh up Richard. Are thy on thi own?"

"Nayew, I'm wi ar Veronica."

"Tha ca knockabart wi us if tha wants."

"O-reight! See yer Vron" We were now a foursome.

We made our way down to the front of the auditorium, picking out four seats together in the third row. As kids, sitting at the front was the best. A hierarchy which was reversed when you became a teenager.

"Duz tha wanna poppet?" Sitting with Richard paid dividends.

For the next ten minutes we jumped over seatbacks, shouted at friends in the balcony, pulled girls' hair, whistled very loud, and made nuisances of ourselves until......the lights went down.

"Wahoooo, Yeaahhhh, Hooraayyyy." The chorus was deafening, then – 'The Warner Brothers' Theme'

Steve with godparents John and Bridie Challoner at his first communion in 1962

"Da-da-dat dat-da-da-da-da da-dat-dat-daaaa..." And we were off on a magical journey. Captured by the allure of the big screen and all its magic.

The film that day was "Go-Kart-GO" starring Dennis Waterman, about a kid with a go-kart (surprisingly) who overcomes many obstacles to become the local champion. Maybe a touch formulaic.

When I got home I was gonna make a trolley (as we called them) and nothing would stop me becoming the local champion, except maybe the fact that we didn't have a local championship.

Gee'or Ruwerin

As we ran out at the end, we leapt, dived, fenced, bow'n'arrowed, flew, lazered and copied every other piece of action we'd seen on the screen that morning. I drove up Wordsworth in a pretend trolley, swerving to avoid obstacles and expertly adjusting my crash helmet and goggles. The bollards outside the doctors became a chicane, and I spent my last penny on a cane which would be my sword.

"Mam, it wor great. This kid 'ad this trolley, an thi wor these burglars, an 'e found the di-monds but 'is trolley got smashed up, but it warn't a trolley, it wor a go-kart..."

Mum did me a cup of tea and listened intently as I poured out the morning's itinerary, in-between slurps, running the whole gamut from Elmer Fudd through to "Satan's Satellites" and asking the occasional pointed question ("Isn't that the boy who plays William on the TV?") to show she was paying attention.

Afterwards we met up on the field and re-enacted as many battles as we could remember, but memory is fickle, and we were soon back to being the TV heroes of the day. I was Mike Mercury. Senna was Steve Zodiac. Kenny was Troy Tempest and Wriggo was Torchy.

The Bush family outside no. 387 in 1974 (Steve's second from left)

Gee'or Ruwerin

Chapter Seven

Country dancing in Grenoside

One of the annual events that plagued my early school years, but on reflection stands out as a beacon of idyllic childhood, was Grenoside Gala Day.

Each year, in the early spring we would start rehearsing. We would traipse into the school hall every Tuesday morning, the girls a little more eagerly than the boys, and line up so that "Miss" could size us off, a bit like they do in the army.

"Christopher! Stop jostling Gillian like that."

"Richard, you are not taller than Anthony."

We would form into two rows, the girls in front, the boys standing gingerly behind. Whichever girl stood directly in front of you, was your partner, at least for that session. This was a traumatic moment. If it was the right girl you were walking on clouds for the next few hours, smiling like a Goon. The wrong girl and – oh dear, you were the subject of your mates' mickey taking for the rest of that day and beyond.

"Nah then Tommy, Bushy's got Goffy ageea'n. Bushy, tha loves Goffy!!"

"Wey, that's berra then lovin Benjo."

For the initial sessions, the school's music teacher played the piano as accompaniment, clanking away on a slightly out of tune Kemble, but as the big day drew closer the school would get copies of the tunes on vinyl, and we danced along as these were played through the tinny horned speaker, "Nipper" conspicuous by his absence.

"An't ye got no Beatles miss? Worrabaht t'Rollin Stoo-erns?"

I can't remember the titles of actual dances but they all had very rustic names like "Tumbledown Jig" and "Gypsy Promenade", and consisted of moves like "Dip-Dive", "Figure 8" and "Up and Double-Back", terms which even now send a shudder down my spine. "Gay Gordon" of course didn't have the connotations then that it does now, or we'd have never gotten through it.

These rehearsals would continue over a few weeks, and eventually we would get the hang of the moves, manage to stifle the ever present giggles, and eventually present some semblance of organised dance.

One or two show offs (ahem!) would even try adding stylish swirls of their own, but these were quickly stamped on by "Miss", not a great believer in individuality.

Then, one fine spring Saturday, we would head up to Greno, joined by teams from all the other "Ecclesfield and District" schools, Mansell, Monteney, Ecco, and all the kids with big foreheads from Lound.

We would be dressed in white shirts, red ties, grey trousers (short, of course!) and white pumps.

The girls wore white frocks and had red ribbons in their hair.

The Village Green, behind the old chapel, was laid out so that the various troupes could line up in formation, with ropes dividing one section from the next.

Gee'or Ruwerin

This was necessary as the "Morris Dancers" were also present, doing their usual stick-bashing and bottle-top waggling, and one school even had a gymnastic display – riveting!

Having rehearsed to records, it always came as a big shock to find that the music on the day was being played live by a live brass band, and so the tempos were a bit different from those in our heads.

We soon however got used to this, and at the opening "DA-DAAH!" from the band, we would bow to our partners and skip off to our prescribed routines, with "Miss's" barked orders ("Up and Double Back!", "Skip down the Aisle!" "Step and Hop, Step and HOP!!!") frittering through our tiny minds at a deadly pace.

Despite the torture of rehearsal, I seem to remember the actual performance as being very enjoyable, heaving a collective sigh of relief when it was over. The applause from the locals was always jolly and enthusiastic, and we all bowed energetically, milking it for all we were worth. Some parents would be there (my own Mom usually showed up) but most kids were orphans for the day.

After performing, we were each given a voucher for a free ice-cream from the local Manfredi's van, the mainstay of any summer outdoor event, and if we added an extra penny we got a "99", covered in lovely gooey raspberry syrup. And of course, it didn't matter if some spilt on your shirt, 'cause the ordeal was now over.

Chapter Eight

Getting' an 'aircut

"Stephen, I think you need a haircut."

These words sent a cold shiver down my spine. I hated getting a haircut for a number of reasons, but mostly because the barber's shop was a torture chamber. Growing up on Wordsworth, my local barber was Varney on Buchanan Rd, a place to be avoided at all costs.

"I don't mum. Skoyl sez we can ave it a bit longer naah cuss o't Beatles."

The first issue was queuing...

The bell rang as I opened the door, and eight faces turned as one to stare.

"Sit dahn thee-er Bushy an don't mek no noise or ah'll githee a clip."

Varney's attitude was that kids went to the back of the queue, made no noise, and didn't fidget

I sat there for hours waiting until all the grown ups had been done and it was my turn. When I was nearly at the front a couple of regular guys came in, and I sunk down to the back of the line.

When eventually my turn came, the fun really started. Varney stuck the plank across the chair arms even though I didn't need it, just to show how insignificant I was, and when I sat on it, I had to bend my neck down to see myself in the mirror.

Once in the chair, the man then wrapped a huge army surplus bed sheet, white with three blue stripes down the middle, around my neck and shoulder, effectively pinning my arms to my side so that, if my nose should happen to start itching (what am I saying IF?? It started itching like billie-oh straight away) I had to perform a Jack Douglas type manoeuvre to try and scratch it, resting my elbow on my knee then jerking it upwards so that my hand came in contact with the offending nostril, giving very temporary relief. Varney of course grunted at this and looked at me in the mirror as if I was something stuck to the bottom of his shoe.

"Can you tilt your head forward please?"

This was a phrase that they didn't teach at barbers' school in those days.

Instead he pumped the chair up with his foot, throwing me off guard. Then he rested his hand on my neck and shoved my head forward in a single jerk, applying a hand -brake so that it came to a stunned stop when it reached the desired position, causing my brain to crash against my forehead. For about the next three minutes my head spun, there were spots before my eyes, and my nose itched like a radio active hot spot. Then, when the mist slowly cleared, I saw in the mirror that the damage had been done.

"I said square neck! Not short back'n'sides!" Nearly in tears at this point.

"Sorry, I forgot."

One of his great skills was that he could cut hair to any given style, as long as it was short back'n'sides.

Gee'or Ruwerin

It didn't matter what you asked for – "Can I have a trim on top, with the sideburns squared off just below the ear, and the back tapered to a point in the neck please?" – You got the regular short back'n'sides.

When the kids in my class began wearing their hair slightly longer, and everyone wanted to look like Pete Howe, I had a barnet straight from a 1940s John Mills film. If someone had pinned a label on my coat and put me on a train, I'd have ended up living in a Welsh farmhouse for three years, with a woman with too many brooms.

And of course it didn't finish with the humiliating haircut. As he was unwrapping the shroud, he recited his famous line.

"Would you like cream?"

I quickly screamed: "No! Please! Not the cream. Not – The – Creeamm!!"

It was already too late. His hands, covered in a thick green slimy shampoo-resistant Palmolive gel, came down on the top of my skull, and plastered my hair into a meringue of mediocrity. As I risked one eye to see the destruction in the mirror, a giant sob welled up in my throat. I knew that for the next week or so, I would look like an absolute numpty. Even the kids from Foxhill would be able to take the mick.

And as it was a few days away from bath night, then the loose hairs on my back and neck gave me itchyjip for some time to come, making it all in all, a nightmare experience.

The Bush clan in 196

24

Chapter Nine

Mekkin' Dens

Living quite close to the filling station on Wordsworth (we knew it simply as "The Garage") it wasn't unusual to have a den located in an actual garage. If some idiot accidentally left one unlocked then it became a free for all.

I remember one year when we discovered one of the "top" garages (Chaucer Rd) unlocked, I think it was number 54. There were also a couple of abandoned vehicles, a Hillman Imp and an old ice cream truck – not Mick Smith's though.

About 5 or 6 of us systematically ripped everything out of the cars that would move, and carried it all, Indian canoe style, over to our new den. We laid the bench seats out down the two sides, and put a driver's seat from the truck next to the compulsory workbench.

" Bungi, can tha get t'steerin whee-el aht?"

"Nayew – it's glooed in."

"As tha tried geein it a kick?"

"Cooerse I ave. Neely brock mi too-er."

Parson Cross resident 'Eddie Bedstead'

There were some oily carpets around so we laid them out in the centre, which gave a very homely look to the whole affair. All it needed was a vase of flowers.

One of the gang (Deso) went home and got his brother's primus stove, and between the rest of us we rustled up some tea bags, milk, sugar, and a couple of chipped cups. In no time at all we were brewing up. We flagged down a Fletchers Feccy van and bought two apple charlottes and two custard. We were tempted to buy a small loaf and see if the stove would toast it, but the money went instead on 5 parkies. It was a real palace, and we were lords of the manor.

It didn't take long for others to find out (how does that happen - is it some form of childhood telepathy?) and we had guys off Fulmere and Margetson banging on the door. Of course, we only let them in if they knew the password, which we'd just made up on the spot. One of the Eyres twins had a small bottle of whisky which he'd nicked from his dad's cabinet, so he was allowed in, and JH came in too, cause she was a girl and who knew where that would lead?

For the next two or three days this was our home, and I would jump out of bed early so as to get a comfy seat. I don't think my mum noticed the missing bottle of milk, and what with the stuff that the other guys brought we ate and drank to our heart's content.

Then - Calamity!!

We turned up one morning and all our stuff had been thrown out onto the driveway, and the garage now had two padlocks on it. Finding a patch of window not covered

Gee'or Ruwerin

in grime, and looking through, we could see that there was now a car on the spot that belonged to us. Worst of all, Deso's primus was still on the workbench, where we'd left it after a leisurely cup of Oxo the previous day.

It was with a heavy heart that we trudged off in search of new adventures, but I'm sure we found plenty.

Chapter Ten

Rounders

"…and this afternoon, instead of the boys playing football and the girls playing netball, we'll all be playing rounders…"

"Oh no Miss – not rahnders. It's a girls' game!"

"It may be that Philip, but none the less, that's what we'll be playing!"

And with that the matter was closed. We knew it was coming. The date and location for the Rounders Cup had just been announced, and as Tommy More's always put a team in, we knew that this year would be no exception. Add to this the fact that the football season was now over, and we had no escape route.

I was personally quite pleased as I actually enjoyed rahnders, but I'd never own up to that in front of my mates.

After lunch, Miss sent me and Tommy to the sports store (it was a cupboard) to fetch the rounders stuff, and we waddled on to the pitch, arms full of sticks, bats, balls and everything else we could carry.

"Right, who's going to bowl?"

"Patrick Miss!!!" The response was as one. Pat had shown his bowling skills the previous year, and his left-handedness made him all the more difficult to bat against.

"Anyone for backstop?"

A few hands went up but Christopher's was keenest so he got the role.

"That's good. Stephen you go on to first base" (Yesss!!)

Thus with a skeletal field we began lining up the rest of the class to bat. The boys all pushed to the front of the queue but Miss made them go back, and so it started with Gillian, Bridget, Angela, Angela and so on.

Pat had been told to reduce his speed a bit, to encourage the girls to try and hit the ball, and one or two did. Susan put it right down near the fence with what would have easily been a rounder in a proper game.

As the boys lined up to bat, Patrick put his foot on the gas, and the Bowler/Back-Stop/Base triangle kicked in. We were soon spreading the ball about quickly, and got nearly all the boys out first ball.

Boy were we good! And this was our first practise session.

By the time of the tournament, we had shaped up into a decent team, and were quite looking forward to it.

I was made captain, and was the proudest kid for miles around

The rules were fairly simple. Ten people in each team, five boys and five girls.

A half rounder was two points, a full rounder four points. That was it really

There were eight schools taking part, so we had a straight knock out. Eight down to four down to two.

Gee'or Ruwerin

First up we were against our local rivals Mansell. They had beaten us in the corresponding football final, so there was a bit of history. Not only that, but three of the team were my best mates, so it was doubly important to win, and win we did.

We batted second and dismissed them for two and a half rounders (ten points), a score which we passed with six people still in, including Susan and another girl.

In the semi-final, we were drawn against hosts Ecco, and so had to put up with the support of about a hundred kids cheerin' for our opponents. But it was to no avail. We scored sixteen points (I got a rounder) and then bowled them out for a measly two points, putting us through to the final.

In the last game we came up against Lound.

They were an unknown quantity. All the other schools were based on or around The Cross, and we all knew each other. But Lound was up High Green, and in those days High Green was a separate village, well removed from us townies.

Lound had powered their way to the final, crushing Mansell B and Monteney on the way, and had amassed more points than us. So it was not without trepidation that we went into bat the final.

From the first ball we knew we were in trouble.

They had a girl bowling, which was almost unheard of, but boy could she get some speed up. I was up first and managed to just get a nick on the ball as it whizzed past me, taking it out of the reach of the back-stop and allowing me a gentle jog to first base. (First base only for a back hit)

By the time I got back to base there were only four of us left in. Susan got a good hit and reached second base scoring two points. Then Richard did the same. I got round without scoring, only to see Susan caught at long-field while trying for a rounder. I then got a half rounder, and enabled Richard to have another bat, but he missed the ball completely and the back-stop bounced the ball in the base ending our innings.

Our school rounders team in 1963 - we were Ecclesfield and District champions (Steve third from right on top row)

Gee'or Ruwerin

Six measly points. They would pass that in no time. We were pig sick. It was the football final all over again.

During the break Miss got our little bowling triangle together and gave us a good pep talk. "Keep your heads up, you can still win this" and a few other clichés, so that we went out determined to give them a run for their money.

We had a little warm up practise, and the ball flew from hand to hand to hand quickly, and suddenly we saw a bit of light.

The Lound team lined up to bat. Bowler first, as was tradition. She looked the part but Patrick's ball flew past her and, via the back-stop, finished up in my hands before she'd even started running. Keeping the momentum going we got through everyone's first bat conceding only two points, and whittled them down to four batters.

As my counterpart, the first base, swung at the ball, he thwacked it and sent it

Family friends Kevin and Lynn O'Kane

over the head of our second base, Gillian. It was rescued by Angela who got it back to the bowler, but not before they'd made second base. They now had four points. We whittled the rest of the team out and so the first base came back to the batting square as last man. It was all or nothing for him. We moved all our fielders out, keeping just the triangle team close in. A rounder would be a disaster to us. Second base would mean a draw, and then some kind of play off. That was no good. We had to get him out.

Patrick toyed with ball, tossing it between his hands, as the batter took his place and crouched down, his right arm extended and the solid bat flickering menacingly. Both back-stop and I were on tenterhooks. Cometh the hour and all that.

Patrick took a step forward and swung his arm viciously forward, releasing the ball at optimum point, and sending it hurtling towards the batter, who swung wildly in an all or nothing manner, and missed. The back-stop blinked, surprised to find the ball in his hands, but recovered in time to throw it to me at first base. I saw it coming in slow motion, and put my hands out to capture it. Thud! It smacked into my hands, and with my foot on the base, we'd won!!

When I collected the cup a few minutes later, the lady presenting it, a councillor from Wortley, had the grace to point out that we were the smallest school in the competition, and had reached the football final two months earlier, as well as winning today. I wanted to take the cup home, but Miss insisted on taking it back to school

The next day, at morning assembly, we were all lined up on the stage and given a rousing round of applause. It didn't quite make up for losing the footie, nothing ever would, but it was highly enjoyable for all that.

Gee'or Ruwerin

Chapter Eleven

"Some people are on the pitch"

The long summer holidays were fast approaching, and this time around they would bring an end to my primary school days. Me and three others, all girls, had passed the 11 pluss and had been accepted in to Grammar.

I was a bit worried. The secondary school was on the doorstep and would have been but a ten minute walk each morning. Grammar however meant a journey across town and two bus-rides. I wanted to tell my mom that I didn't really fancy it, but just two weeks after my eleventh birthday, I didn't have the words.

Then there was the uniform. All my mates would be able to wear ordinary clothes to school, but I would have a full green and yellow outfit, including a twirly piping on the blazer cuffs, sold exclusively at Cole Brothers.

There was a big plus though - Football. The school's football teams were among the very best in Sheffield, and I knew that if I got into the team, then I would be playing twice a week for most of the school year.

Since the beginning of the present school-year, way back in September, I, along with most of the other boys in my class, had been taken over by a love of football.

It's normal for boys of ten or eleven to develop a passion for the game, but this year there were three key factors which inflated the palaver:

1.1 Reason 1 - The School Team

St Thomas More's was a small school.

The entire J4 was made up of just 14 boys, and 12 girls, so to have eleven reasonably good players (boosted by two very good players from J3) was a real blessing. I had been an automatic selection for the team, and had even been considered for the captaincy, although I was quick to admit that the right lad got the job.

Add to this the fact that one of Sheffield Wednesday's reserve

St Thomas More Football Team in May 1966. Steve Bush standing proud (middle - back row) after they achieved Ecclefield and District runners up position

players,Tom McAnearny, who lived just a short walk from the school's lovely greenfield site in Grenoside, had agreed to come to the school each week, and coach the lads. Thanks to his enthusiasm and tactical guidance, the team reached the final of the Ecclesfield and district primary schools' knock-out, just losing out to neighbours Mansell after extra time. Although heartbroken by the defeat, my love of the game became ingrained, and I would come to know its ups and downs well in the next few months.

Gee'or Ruwerin

1.2 Reason 2 - The FA Cup Final

From day one, I had supported Sheffield United, and by the age of eleven had watched them play on half-a-dozen occasions. I could name the entire team, and in Keith Kettleborough, had an idol to follow, and so, like many other Unitedites, I was torn in two when city rivals Wednesday, reached the FA Cup Final.

My dilemma? To support Wednesday through the game, or not.

The final was always a big occasion, and there was no room for neutrals, but, without ever making a conscious decision, I found myself cheering for Wednesday, even wearing the free blue-and-white paper hat which came in the Daily Express. When subsequently, the Owls surrendered a two goal lead and lost 3-2, my heartbreak was genuine, and I shed many tears, as I had two weeks earlier when Tommy More's had lost.

1.3 Reason 3 - The World Cup Finals

Most English people are aware that England hosted, and in fact won, the World Cup Finals that year.

Geoff Hurst's hat-trick has been shown, and continues to be shown, many many times on TV. The phrase "They think it's all over" is as much a part of English heritage, as say "We shall fight them on the beaches" or "Geeooer ruwerin or al githee summet to ruwer abaht... "

What is less well documented is how, during the finals, the whole country went really football mad. Most fifty year old housewives could have picked out Bobby Charlton, in a line up. Pele and Eusebio were as familiar to schoolgirls as Paul McCartney and Eden Kane were. Even the tiger tails, normally given away free at Esso garages with four gallons, had been replaced by small, half-crown type coins, displaying bad likenesses of Jimmy Greaves and Terry Paine.

I therefore, football-madder than most, had been delighted when, on my 11th birthday, Mr Chapman from next door, had given me a ticket for the West Germany v Switzerland game at Hillsborough. Bill himself, a life long Sunderland supporter who had settled in Sheffield after the war, would be taking me.

As we queued up for the number 49, the excitement was mounting. As well as us, the bus shelter was full of match-ticket holders, many of them wearing blue-and-white or red-and-white scarves, and when the bus arrived, we squeezed on downstairs and had to stand. It seemed that the whole of Parson Cross was going to the game, and the atmosphere on the bus was electric. Kevin O'Kane was even trying to get everyone to sing England songs, but it didn't really work.

When we got off the bus, we made our way through heavy crowds along Penistone Road, and down Vere Road, to the Leppings Lane end. There were a few Swiss and German supporters mixed in with, and outnumbered by, the locals, and the mounted police kept control from their high perches.

Outside the ground, Mr Chapman queued to get hot-dogs, and as I waited I counted the newly erected flagpoles along Penistone Rd, displaying the flags of all the competing countries. I was even able to recognise a few.

When the hot-dogs came, I asked

"Why are there only fifteen?"

Gee'or Ruwerin

Mr Chapman, trying to avoid a mustard spillage, didn't quite get the question, and his face displayed puzzlement.

"Flagpoles" I explained. "There are sixteen teams, but only fifteen flagpoles. Why?"

"Well I dinaah Stephen" Mr Chapman, sounding like the likely lads now that he was in relaxed mode, glanced across to the display. "Perhaps one got knocked doon or summink."

"No, if you look you can see, there's only ever been fifteen. There isn't room for another one."

" Maybe one got nicked. Should I tell a coppa Stephen?" Mr Chapman was smiling now.

"No, it doesn't matter" My interest was waning and I wanted to get into the ground. I munched my hot-dog as I went off through the "juvenile" turnstile, meeting up with Mr Chapman on the other side.

As we walked up the gangway, two girls in Swiss national costume were handing out small Swiss-flags-on-sticks to everyone. I took two from the girl and asked her if she could yodel?

"Nayew, burra can sing Summer 'Oliday" she returned in a laughing Barnsley accent.

When we took our place on the terrace, about six rows from the front, we could see, through all the waving Swiss flags, that the opposite end of the ground had been issued with German flags. By girls from Chesterfield, I reckoned.

Anyway, as this was the Swiss end, I would be supporting Switzerland.

When the teams emerged onto the pitch, the Swiss team, in red and white, ran across to our end of the ground, causing much cheering and flag waving from the local 'Swiss' contingent. The players waved back to the masses, and a few of them even came and shook hands with those at the front. During the kick about, one of the balls landed in the crowd close to me and I tried to touch it, but couldn't quite reach.

Then the teams were then called into the centre, and lined up for the national anthems.

As the German anthem played, many of the older supporters, including Mr Chapman, looked anxious and shook their heads. The German team, in white shirts and black shorts, stood rigid to attention, and all sang the stirring song. There was

SWFC fans outside the New Inn in Wadsley Bridge in 1966 as they prepare for the trip to the FA Cup final at Wembley

Gee'or Ruwerin

some mild booing, and I supposed that this came from "Swiss" fans, wanting their team to win.

Once the game kicked off however, it was obvious they weren't going to.

Germany controlled the whole game from start to finish. Two of their players, Haller, who looked like the German boy in The Hotspur, and Overath, were superb. They destroyed the Swiss defence, running at them with the ball, switching wings, and tying their opponents in knots. It was the first time I had seen ball control demonstrated so openly. One stood on the ball, the other swung his foot over it. They even back-heeled it to players they couldn't see. They were masterful, and helped their team to a 5-0 victory, after being three up at half time. The Swiss were gallant but out of their depth, and sportingly applauded their supporters at the end.

After the game, milling through the crowds on their way back to the bus-stop, I picked up a discarded German flag, and that night I arranged a criss-cross of Swiss/German flags on my bedroom bookcase.

I told my mum, and anyone else who would listen, that Germany were going to win the competition, and I even took my spare Swiss flag to school and gave it to Miss Griffiths, who knew all about geography.

At tea time the following day, as I was watching Fireball XL5, mum got up to answer a knock at the door, and came back into the front room followed by Mr Chapman, who smiled at me and said "North Korea".

Puzzled but polite, I repeated. "North Korea?"

"Yes, North Korea."

Realising that I was baffled, he went on to explain.

"The missing flagpole is North Korea."

"Ohh." The penny was now dropping "North Korea..." I nodded my head.

"..Why?"

"Well," Mr Chapman explained "Since the war in Korea, the British government refuses to recognise North Korea as a country, only South Korea. So they can't fly their flags."

I thought a moment.

"Well that's daft..." Wisdom beyond my years.

I conjured up a mental image of two girls from Darlington, stood at one end of Middlesbrough's Ayresome Park, in North Korean national dress, handing out empty sticks.

"Do they play the anthem?" I asked.

"I shouldn't have thought so", mam interjected.

I felt sorry for the little Korean players. Millions of miles from home and not able to sing "God Save the Emperor" or whatever. I vowed to cheer extra hard for them in their next televised game.

"Well, that's as maybe Mrs Bush, I must get back for my tea now".

No sign of Terry Collier today, and to me he said "I just thought I'd let you know."

"Bye Mr Chapman" me and mum said together

"And thanks for takin' me to t'match last night" I finished, as Mr Chapman, smiling, went out through the door.

Chapter Twelve

The dreaded Eleven Plus

At the age of eleven, or ten in my case, it was time to take the dreaded eleven plus.

On reflection it seems that my passing the exam was something of a formality. My brothers had all passed and I had a reasonable grasp of sums and reading. My mum always spoke of me going to De La Salle as a foregone conclusion.

For me though it was less certain, and there were a number of variables to consider:

Firstly, I didn't want to go to De La Salle. It was a long bus ride. It smelled of formaldehyde (it did, I'm not kidding!) and my godfather was the school caretaker. Don't get me wrong, he was a lovely guy, a sort of gentle Irish giant, but I didn't want him that close when I was getting into trouble.

"Aah sure now Stephen, I'm sure your mummy wouldn't be too pleased to know about that!"

Secondly, it was very religious. It was run by (sort of) priests. I was growing out of religion and I didn't want it rammed down my throat anymore. It was bad enough with the nuns at junior school. De La Salle brothers were to be avoided at all costs.

Thirdly and most importantly. None of my mates would be there! Within 50 yards of my house I had half-a-dozen good mates, and I wasn't willing to give that up just for the sake of a decent education. (Over the years this argument has lost its conviction!)

When I was taking the "eleven-plus", there was a distinction made between "Sheffield" pupils and "West Riding" pupils.

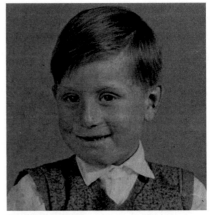

My 1963 school photo

The two groups of kids took different exams in different locations. As a West Riding kid I had to go to Monteney School to take mine. Sheffield kids went somewhere else, Mansell I think.

The geographical dividing line between the two was the same as the the Parson Cross/New Parson Cross border, which was the dike, which runs across Wordsworth just down from the Close, under what is now the filling station.

When I was a kid the surface of the road changed at that point from tarmac to concrete, as it came under a different maintenance region. The streetlamps also changed. Sheffield had the Green "Dixon of Dock Green" lamps while West Riding had the new fabricated concrete lights. Posh, we were. Although, 80 years after the

Gee'or Ruwerin

death of Sherlock Holmes, we stilled referred to them as Gaslamps, or "Gassies".

On the day, me and a group of girls who lived in Grenoside and Ecclesfield, made our way down to Monteney in a small group, and after nervously wandering into the school hall ('scuse me. Are they dooin't eleven plus ere?), were eventually given seats at the front. The Monteney kids were also there for the big test.

My memories of the actual test are vague at best. One thing I can recall is a question about the area of a rectangular shape, in square inches. I simply measured it's height and width and multiplied the two. It was only on the walk back to Tommy More's that I realised that most of my friends had been defeated by this.

"What the chuffin 'ell is a square inch? Did that get that 'en Bushy?"

"Nayew" (the lie embarrasses me now more than it did then). "I think tha needs a prer-tractor to do it, an I din't have one."

When the results were announced a few weeks later, I was the only boy in the school to pass. Three girls also passed, but as they went to a separate school, Notre Dame at Ranmoor, they would disappear from my radar very quickly.

Wordsworth Tavern –
still going to this day

Chapter Thirteen

Tongue Gutter

The small river which meanders down the western perimeter of the field from Wordsworth to Holgate is the Tongue Gutter. It changes its name to "Sheffield Lane Dike" at Holgate Ave and then "Hartley Brook" at Barnsley Rd. By all accounts you can now get guided tours along it, but I guess that at the age of nine or ten nobody knew that river better than we did

During those long summer school breaks we would often play for the whole day around "Our Stream" (it didn't have a name to us). We knew the best place to get a jar of taddies after spawning time. We could also get hold of a few sticklebacks, especially when it had been raining for a while, and the area down around Deerlands garages became marshy. And we became experts at the long jump. We could identify all the places where, if you were leaping to and fro across the stream, it suddenly became wide enough to be a bit of a challenge, and eventually there would be a spot where you had to make an extra special leap, or suffer the consequences. Falling in was an occupational hazard, and I recall often having to either go home and face the wrath or, more likely, spend two hours running my clothes dry. I genuinely thought that mum wouldn't notice that I was caked in dried mud. She did.

My strongest memory though is of the days when we went on expeditions through the "tunnels". Going under Holgate was fairly easy, It was not much wider than the road and you could always see the "light at the end of the tunnel". Most of the mardys could manage that, and occasionally even a girl would go through. The coolest thing to do was to stop halfway through, perch precariously to one side in a tenuous sitting position, and have a fag. When cars went over your head, it was like a very small earthquake, or so we thought. A bus was about "six" on the Richter scale.

A bigger challenge though, was going under Wordsworth, in the small opening next to Roy Fox's. This went under the Wordsworth garage site, then up under Chaucer garages, and continued on up towards Foxhill. Every so often was a "Sitting". This was where there was a grate above your head, and the stepped sides formed a welcome seat. You could even stand at this point. Lighting a candle and a Woodbine flip was now the order of the day, and there was evidence of others having previously enjoyed a similar leisure trip. Around the second sitting, the light at the opening would drift out of sight, and here the claustrophobics would have a field day, hiding their fears by telling tales of impending doom. The rest of us would go as far as the fourth sitting, but that was probably as adventurous as we could manage. We always came back down at a hundred miles an hour, and it was blessed relief to breathe fresh air again. I often wondered if the world had changed while I'd been potholing. Been watching too much Dr Who I guess.

Yep, if you want a guided tour of the Tongue Gutter, my twelve year old alter ego is the expert.

Gee'or Ruwerin

Chapter Fourteen

At the seaside

"Stephen!"

Mum's shout was quite loud and it echoed on the stairs.

Oh flippin 'eck. Worrava dun nah??

"What?"

"There's a present here for you from Mr Carr."

Woosh! I was down them stairs like lightning. It was normal on Saturdays that I went back to bed after my "papper rahnd" and had a few hours extra kip, but if a present came then that changed things.

"Worrizit?"

"Have a look and see."

On the telephone table was a blank white envelope, and mum pointed to it, helpfully. I snatched it up thinking "Money. It's gorra be money" I dug my fingers in and pulled out two small tickets. Holding them up I read eagerly:

"Southey Green Working Men's Club

"Cleethorpes

"Tuesday 15th August

"Coach No 26."

The "26" was stamped on, bigger and paler than the rest.

"Wahoo!! – Ahhm gunna Cleethorpes, Ahhm gunna Cleethorpes" I sang as I danced around the front room, waving the tickets high, and tripping over the cat.

Why this was such a surprise I'm not sure, as Mr Carr gave us club trip tickets every year, but it was always really welcome. His own two kids were grown up now, so I guess me and our Mick were the nearest thing for him and his wife.

One lovely aspect of growing up in Parson Cross, was the Working Men's Club Trip. Although the clubs had their issues, and certainly corruption was often mentioned, here was an act of true benevolence.

It was an annual event, usually taking place on a Tuesday in early August. The build up would consist of two or three weeks in which tickets were feverishly sought, bought, and exchanged. Coach numbers were critical, and it took a number of swaps before you and your mates were all on the same bus.

"As anyone gorra sixteen forra number 9?"

Low numbers were prestigious, though truth be told it made precious little difference.

The day started early. I met up with my mates at the bus stop, and jumped on the 49 as it came round the island, sitting next to all the Bassetts and Fletchers women, smoking and gossiping their way down Wordsworth Avenue, their white turbans a proud badge of community.

Gee'or Ruwerin

"Ahr Cliff's off ter't chuffin seaside fo't day an' Ahr've gorra spend eight howers on't chuffin feccy counter."

As I got off the bus, I could see the magnificent sight of thirty-plus charabancs lined up on Southey Green Road. The first few were all in the beautiful green livery of Law Brothers, the others a mixed bag of size and colour, each proudly displaying its "On Hire To Law Bros" sign, alongside the crucial bus number. The street was lined with stewards loading crisps, pop and beer on to the coaches, kids still trying to get a swapsie for their pal's chara, ("anybody gorra 33 forra 17??") and mums, bidding their charges farewell before going home for a rare day of peace.

We sat quite near the back, allowing the freedom of being distant from the steward, and enabling a few crafty Woodbines to be passed around. As it was summer, many of the coaches had previously been used for fishing trips, so the predominant smell was Bream Snot. It was also common to share the back seat with a large family of maggots (I'm sure they did it on purpose) as cleaning the bus was the driver's responsibility, and few of them went overboard. After the usual hustle and bustle that goes with thirty-five excited kids, and a few verbal warnings from the stewards about behaviour (No Smoking? Yeah, that'll be right) the vehicles pulled away, one by one, and set off on the road to that great tourist haven, the Venice of the East Midlands, Cleethorpes.

Getting to Cleethorpes these days is a doddle. 90 minutes max on the motorway and you fall of the end of it into Grimsby, in 1968 it was so different. The convoy wound its way through South Yorkshire housing estates, which in turn gave way to leafy Lincolnshire lanes. People waved at us (Honest! They really did) as we snaked though their quaint little villages, and we of course waved back, not yet brave enough to do moonies. There was a halfway stop, a small transport cafe that served snacks and drinks. The main objective of course was the toilet, which was ankle deep in fluid by the time the fourth coach had gone through. There was a juke box playing the hits of the day, and whenever I hear Death of a Clown by Dave Davies (Where's Brian Matthew's Knighthood, that's what I want to know!!) I am back in that little sticky bun bar. The garden next door had a small orchard, and one lad from near The Fortyfoot pub got back on the bus, his pockets bulging with small sour apples, which were almost uneatable. I say almost because of course we did eat them, and threw the cores at the locals as we resumed our invasion of their sleepy hollows.

Once we set off again, the steward set about his most important task. Doling out the spendo! This was the high spot of the day, as a guy with a big bag of half-crowns came towards you, and picked out three (yes, three!!) for each kid.

"'ere thy art Bushy. Don't spend it all on Park Drive, heh heh heh."

"Thanks mester Ashton, nah I can affooerd to get mi mam a stick o rock."

I'd managed to con a further 2/6 out of my mum, and that meant a total of ten bob!! All that dosh! Luxury

Arrival in Cleethorpes was signalled by a long traffic jam, as the parking attendants tried to shoehorn two-thirds of Sheffield's coach corps into the Victoria car park. The steward then delivered his well rehearsed lines about lunch, displaying your badges, not getting lost, and making sure you were back on the bus by six sharp or it would leave without you, (for Angela Sellars that very nearly came true) then we were free. Free to roam the streets (street?) of Cleethorpes, armed with just half-a-quid and a lunch voucher for the Victoria cafe.

"Come on Wriggo" Race thi ter't beearch!"

"Can't. Ah've got ahr Brians wellos on."

The events of the day were many and varied. I have memories of the Big Dipper (small as it turns out), donkeys, rifle-ranges, carousels, hot-dogs, brandy snaps (what a disappointment they were!), snogging, and top ten hits blaring out from the tinny speakers of the fast moving rides. (Sweets for my sweet. Sugar for my hunee).

My favourite item was the laughing policeman. This was a 1940s mannequin with paint peeling from its face, dressed in ill-fitting uniform, and sat in a glass case. When I put a penny in, it rocked back and forth to the accompaniment of the song, The Laughing Policeman. Stephen King must have seen this, as I'm sure it was the inspiration for about eight of his books. Scary doesn't cover it. I still have nightmares to this day, and if I'm being particularly mischievous, my wife threatens me with that song.

Lunch was an absolute bun fight. Hundreds of ill-mannered brats shovelling fish and chips down their cakeholes. (Grimsby Fish, soaked in vinegar. Now there's a memory to cherish.) Nicking the ketchup off the next table before they had finished with it. "Nah then, ave yer gorr-any 'enderson's?". Holding the salt cellar upside down and blowing the salt in a girl's face. (Boy, was I cool). Flicking peas at Wriggo and Senna. It was brilliant. The staff must have dreaded it. I can only imagine it must have taken ages to get the place back to normal.

Round about 5 o'clock, the seven and a tanner long spent, we congregated around the bus park, meeting up with others off our coach who we'd not seen all day.

"Wot yore been dooin? We'v 'ad six guz on't dipper."

"We gorra snog offern some lasses from Wood'ouse."

"Bet yer did. Donkeys moo-er like."

"We did. Yer can ask ahr Dave."

As the crowds built up, eventually the driver and steward came, each carrying a crate of Long Life, and unlocked the door. One by one we filed on, less excited now, positively weary, and slumped into a seat ready for the long journey back. At ten past six, the other charas long gone, Angela Sellars turned up, refusing to say what she'd been up to, but looking disheveled and red faced. Then, as an air of calm swept around the coach, the journey home began. Some brave soul would try to get a sing along going, {Bye Bye Blackbird, but NOT the Black and White Minstrels version} and there was a dare to try and nick a Long Life, but it didn't amount to anything.

After a short uncomfortable sleep, Barnsley appeared on the road signs, and then, like some modern day Xanadu, Parson Cross materialised before my very eyes, and we were at the club. The walk back up Wordsworth was full of animated conversation, about what we'd done, whom we'd snogged, and what Angela Sellars had actually been up to. Then home. A nice cup of tea, Late Night Line Up, bed, and the first of many nocturnal visits from the Laughing Policeman.

Chapter Fifteen

"Spud Pickin"

At the age of 12, myself and a group of pals arranged with a farmer on Salt Box Lane, to work picking his spuds for a week. It was probably in early October. My mates, who were all at Yew Lane, actually had a week off, which was officially called "Spud Pickin' Week". I was at De La Salle and was afforded no such luxury (I guess my middle class schoolmates didn't need the money like I did) so me and Terry Glaves had to wag it for the week.

We got up early and met at the top of the jennel. Memory says there were six of us, but that's by no means assured. We passed around a Park Drive to get us in the mood as we walked up Knutton, the lighted tip glowing bright red and burning to a point with all the exaggerated inhaling. We thought about having a sing-song but it never quite materialised.

When we passed The Beagle, Joe's wife waved at us through the window as she hoovered the curtains in the best room.

There was an animated discussion about whether we should walk up the cinder path or head straight along Creswick Lane. The cinder path won. Halifax Road was really busy at this time of the morning, and we watched the cars, pointing out any that looked flash or sounded souped up, zoom past on their way to town.

When we reached the farm we got a lovely surprise. There was a big industrial sized pot of tea waiting for us, and as we guzzled it down the farmer's wife brought out a tray of bacon sandwiches. We couldn't believe it!! This was before we'd even started.

While we munched down the sarnies, the farmer and his driver gave us a run down of what was going to happen. Basically we would follow the churner as it ploughed up the field, grab the tatties as they became visible, and pile them into the buckets provided. There was a few safety rules but did we listen? Did we eckerslike. It all sounded quite easy and the ten bob per half-day we were getting should be easy money. Wrong!

It all went smoothly at first, and as we grabbed the spuds we laughed and joked and did impressions of local grown-ups such as Eddie Bedstead and Dennis Craggs. One kid even mimicked Mrs Williams, vacuuming the pub curtains with her nose in the air as if avoiding a nasty smell. After a very short while though, it became obvious that the spring had gone out of our steps, and that what we were doing was actually very hard work. Bending down became a real chore, and at the grand old age of twelve I suffered my first bout of backache.

We all managed to make it through to lunchtime when we were rewarded with another round of farm fresh butties, and all the tea we could drink, which was lots.

The farmer even offered to pay off anyone who wanted to quit, but none of us did.

We all struggled through the afternoon, and the stiffness kind of eased up as we reached the end of the day. We each made sure that our names were in the farm notebook, and that £1 was pencilled in against us. Friday seemed so far away, but we already knew we would make it.

The rest of the week continued in much the same vein. At the end of each day we could collect any monies owing, but all chose to accrue. Not an easy thing to do at that time, as none of us had the proverbial two ha'pennies.

As we walked home, passing a Woody around, we sang a few rugby songs we'd picked up from the Army Cadets, ("Dinah Dinah show us yer legs" – that kinda thing) and a selection of current chart hits. The one that springs to mind is "Good News Week" by Hedgehoppers Anonymous, and there was also a Yardbirds song which we all liked.

We walked home the long way, past the top of Foxhill and down by Tommy More's old church. That way, if anyone saw us smoking they'd be less likely to know us.

Come the Friday we were all excited. We'd made good time and our erstwhile employer (we were all calling him "Boss" by this stage) had told us that if we could finish the lower field by lunchtime, no mean feat let me tell you, he would pay us off for the full day.

The Parson Cross site pre-1925

Well you should have seen us. Scampering around like sewer rats, pouncing on anything resembling a chipper. We even had to tell the tractor to go faster as we nearly got caught up in its rotors. It was mayhem, but at about 12:45 we sucked up the last few taytos from the final harrowed groove, and collapsed on the floor with exhaustion. Even the sight of a giant teapot and a mound of sarnies the size of Back-Edge, surrounded by freshly cooked chips, failed to goad us into action, but eventually we crawled on our hands and knees across to the picnic table, and tucked in.

Then it came. Paydirt!!

The boss walked down the path towards us, clutching a worn leather Gladstone bag which would have looked at home in any Charles Dickens film. You could hear the coins jingling from fifty yards away. He plonked the bag on the table and got out his notebook, and began thumbing slowly through the pages (Come On! Erry up!) till he reached the page with our names on. He called us out one by one, and we went up to collect our hard earned cash from him. A bit like the army pay parades I would attend years later. As he paid each guy £5 10/- (Yes! There was a ten bob bonus each!!) he shook hands with us and told us there would be a job next year if we could make it.

Walking home that night was a delight. The singing and laughing was louder than before (it really was Good News Week!) and we stopped off at The Bassett to buy fags. Spurning the usual No 6 Tipped (after all, I was a man of wealth now) I pushed the boat out and bought 20 (yes, 20!) Embassy for 4/6d. Walking on down

Gee'or Ruwerin

Deerlands, I got through about four of them before I reached Chaucer.

We split up at the roundabout and went off in different directions to Wordsworth, Fulmere and elsewhere, each still with a crispy five pound note and some loose change weighing our respective pockets down.

I guess it's difficult to explain to kids today how much that fiver meant. The most I'd ever had was Half-a-Crown, and that was a rarity. I'd never earned money before – okay maybe threepence for going to the shops but I'm not sure that counts – and here I was with a real five pound note, the fruits of a full week's endeavours.

I know it may have been child-labour, and was probably exploitative, but it created one of my very fondest childhood memories, and whenever I hear The Hedge-hoppers, usually on Brian Matthew's Sounds of the Sixties, Saturdays at 8 am on Radio 2 (Where's his knighthood?? Pull your finger out Prime Minister) it reminds me of a few glorious autumnal days and childhood friendships which still endure.

Colley Working Mens Club – late 1980s

Chapter Sixteen

Paper Round

Just after my 13th birthday, I began noticing that I didn't have any money.

I'd not had any previously, but it didn't seem to matter as I didn't really want to buy much other than spice. Now I was looking at Levis, Ben Shermans, Woodbines, and a million other things I couldn't afford.

I toddled up Chaucer Rd and approached Mr Fogg (Harry to his friends and cheeky paperboys) and asked him if he had any jobs going.

"Thy art 14 aren't tha?" I was asked.

"Cooerse I am" I responded, sucking on a woodbine for effect.

"Cum in Sunday morning then, and tha can be 't spare lad - an don't be late."

I was excited come Sunday, and got up as soon as it got light. This being July, that was well before 6 o'clock, and there was no way I was going back to sleep. I hunted around for matching socks (vainly as it turned out), ran a damp flannel over my face, and listened to the radio until 6:30. I then headed up the garden path and across three more shortcuts, on schedule to meet Harry's famous bonus time. (In before 6:45 for six out of seven days got you half-a-crown bonus!!)

I skipped into the shop whistling Gershwin's Foggy Day (I'd just heard Billie Holliday singing it on the Light Programme) only to greeted by my new boss asking.

"Who'er tha?". I'd obviously made a good impression.

"Bushy! – tha genn me a job last week."

He gave a grunt of vague recognition and got me to help him marking-up. This process entailed Harry shouting "No 42. Observer". I would then scamper round, pick an Observer off the pile, and write 42 on the front upper border. Harry knew the habits of the lads, and so we marked-up the rounds in roughly the order the team came in.

The first was "Rocher". This was a small private estate just off the top of Yew Lane, and due to their inflated incomes (I was off Wordsworth don't forget) they all had the Sunday Times, complete with all the magazines and supplements. That bag weighed a ton, and the delivery boy, Pod, split the load into two and waddled up Chaucer, paper bags criss-crossed around his straining neck, ready to face the rigours of schnauzers and French poodles.

The marking-up took us until 8 o'clock, as a steady stream of half-asleep kids came in, picked up their bags and set off for sleepy suburbia, or Mansell Ave as we called it. By half-eight there was one forlorn bag left, sat in the corner trying not to look sad. A card sticking out of it said "Deerlands" and it became apparent that Syd, guardian of the Deerlands circuit, wasn't coming in.

"Weere's tha live Bushbaby?" I kinda knew what was coming.

"Wordsworth."

"Well, tha should know Deerlands alreight. Does tha fancy tekkin sum pappers?"

Gee'or Ruwerin

And so, five minutes later I set off on my debut round.

And I absolutely loved it.

I felt really important making sure that Mrs Heyward got her Sunday Mirror, and delivering a News of the World for the Websters. I went up one side, towards Halifax Rd, detouring around the mount for a single Sunday Post and to be barked at by an alsatian. I then came down the other side, and finished off with the last few on Wordsworth, my own house being the coincidental last stop (it really was). I had a quick cup of tea, nicked a tab-end out of the ashtray (still no-one up) and listened to more kitchen radio. Jack Di Manio was on now, playing a selection of crooners and torch singers from the 50s. Ella came on singing "Everytime we say Goodbye" and it's stuck with me ever since.

Harry had asked me to come back to the shop after I'd finished, and when I did, he gave me my first pay, sixpence for being marker-up and a bob for the round. He also winked at me and slipped me five parkies, then said

"See thee tomorra – an don't be late."

I worked there for over two years, finishing off as head lad, which meant dishing out the Stars to the other guys, and working in the shop if they were short.

It was a great introduction to working life, and I'm sure helped me to appreciate endeavour, and indeed, its rewards.

Dad in his greenhouse

Chapter Seventeen

Throwin' Arrers

"Mam 'ave wi gorrany canes?"

"Canes?" There was that look again.

"Yer, I need a cane."

"A garden cane?"

I began a sarcastic reply along the lines of "no, one o' them living room canes" but then thought better of it.

"Yeah."

I then spent the next ten minutes rummaging around the greenhouse, and going through a pile of canes that dad had used for holding tomatoes up, until I found the ideal candidate. It was about two-and-a-half feet long, with a notch about nine inches from one end.

Using a sharp knife, I split the end with two cuts made at right angles to each other. Then using thin card from a Frosties packet, I made two sets of flights, by carefully folding them, and sliding them down into the cuts in the cane ("Here's one I made earlier!"). I then sealed the gaps between the flights with a good wrapping of sello-tape, and stuck a bit more around the end for good measure.

At the other end (the business end) I knocked a small nail in, to act as a weight. Some of my mates, who worked at EITB, had some very elaborate weights, deadly shards carved on the lathes of apprenticeship, but a nail would do me for now.

I had made my very first throwin' arrer.

I nicked a lace out of a shoe in the porch, and tied a healthy knot in one end, then ran across the road to the field. A number of my pals were already there, launching these deadly missiles into space, and chasing down the path after them.

"Wots tha got thee-er Bushy?"

"Wot's tha think it is?"

"Did tha mekkit thissen?"

"Coo-erse I did."

"Bet thee it dunt fly."

It had better fly or I'd look like a right twerp.

I wrapped the knotted end of the string just above the notch, and, with the other end pulled tight in my hand, I gripped the sharp end, and picked up any excess string with circular hand wraps. I took a few steps back into the road, then ran full pelt towards the field, and just before my feet touched grass, I hurled the arrow in a kind of cricket bowling action, in the direction of Ray Burns' garden.

I got the same kind of thrill that Isaac Newton must have had when he invented gravity. The arrow soared into orbit, spinning like one of Bully's darts, and came back down to earth some 20 yards down the field. It stuck in the earth, and I could

Gee'or Ruwerin

see Tony the Tiger, peering through the long grass at me, waiting for another go.

I quickly retrieved it, and during the next few hours perfected my technique. I was soon able to get it way past the end of Robbo's garden, and easily made 40 or 50 yards.

Some of the older lads had big three-footers, with mild-steel arrowheads that came straight off a cave drawing (usually stuck in a buffalo's back), and up to four flights, smallest one at the notch, biggest at the end. Those guys could really make them fly and it was fascinating to see them gliding over the playing area, and thudding into the ground some 100 yards away.

That summer, it seemed that all we did was throw arrows. Some days we even went to Parson Cross Park and used the football pitches as our ranges. I don't recall anyone ever getting hit by an arrow, the mind boggles at the mere thought, but those long school holidays of 1968 were a memorable time of experiment and enlightenment.

John Bush in action on the 'cycle speedway' track

Gee'or Ruwerin

Chapter Eighteen

Eagles versus Devils

I was just diggin' into my second dish of cornflakes when I heard a Tarzan call from out front of the house.

"Aaaah-Ah-Aaaaaa…"

This was Wriggo's alternative to knocking the front door. I stood at the front window and held up two fingers to show that I wouldn't be long, but he beckoned me with a "Come 'ere" type wave of his arm, urgency showing in his face.

"What's up wi thee?" I swung open the front door

"As tha seen wots appenin on't field?" He shouted across the front garden "Your Bushy an Pete Howe are digging it all up!"

The first thing I thought was that if two teenagers were to dig the field 'all up' then it would take them about 50 years, but if Wriggo claimed it was true, then it would at least have some credence.

"See yer later Mam!" I hopped down the path putting my Wayfinders on as I went, so that by the time I reached Wriggo we were both in full stride and belted across the road together, looking neither right, nor left, nor right again.

As we got to the football pitch, we saw about ten teenage lads, two of my brothers among 'em, digging up the playing area, and arranging the sods in a kind of oval pattern. All the time being watched by four girls, Bee-Bee, Barbara and two others. Wriggo had been spot on.

"Wot your doin'?"

I asked Ray, who was just pushing down on a spade with the sole of his steel-capped boot, knowin' that my brothers would just ignore me

"Wi mekkin a track."

"A runnin track?"

"Nayew yer daft a'peth. A speedway track."

Now call me picky, but a running track would have been slightly more feasible than a speedway track.

"Wot for?"

"So we can do cycle speedway!" Ray was walking away now, balancing a square of turf on his shovel. He placed it on top of a line of others, so that it looked like the pile of sandbags in front of an army trench.

Wriggo and I were really puzzled, each of us having a distinct question mark hovering over our heads, so went and sat with the girls for a laugh.

"Don't gi' em ar phone number", one of my brothers called out, as we sat on the dry summer grass to watch events unfold. (I did though!)

During that summer a 'Cycle Speedway' craze had gone around Sheffield and a few other places. It seemed that everywhere you went, a group of youths was digging

Gee'or Ruwerin

up common land and turning it into a small speedway track.

I was familiar with the real Speedway as I used to go to Owlerton on Thursdays to watch the Tigers. One of my pals' dads was a St John's volunteer, and he used to get "comps" for us most weeks, so we quickly became experts, and could name most of the local riders (Clive Featherby, Jack Kitchen, John Dews). We even got to see international matches, and knew all the top Swedish riders, who seemed to dominate at that time. That lovely smell, a mix of diesel and red shale, is one that will stay with me for life. That, and the sensation

John Bush (left) and Dominic Woodcock perfect their 'cycle speedway' skills

of being pelted with small stones, as the riders come around your curve, their back wheels skidding ominously outwards as they gunned the throttles forward.

"C'mon Clive! Let's av' a Max!!"

I knew the scoring system by heart, and could hold the scores of each player in my head. I could tell at any point which team was in front, and what was needed by the opposition to reverse that.

I could even tell you where the team manager lived and which Sunday newspaper he had, (Observer) 'cause I delivered it...

...but Cycle Speedway? That was a new one on me.

A few weeks later, the track was ready to host its first meeting. No doubt a lot of stuff had gone on behind the scenes, as two teams had been formed, Parson Cross Eagles and Parson Cross Devils, and they had joined a league, but all I had seen had been the training, which took place on those long summer evenings.

The starting gate was a washing pole (no kidding) dug into the bank on the inside of the track, with a length of sturdy knicker elastic tied to it, about 18" off the ground. The starter would pull the laggy band across to the outside of the track, creating a starting line, behind which the competitors lined up. They would each be stood astride their respective bikes, one foot on the front pedal, the other on the ground with the back of the leg pressed firmly against the rear pedal, holding the whole thing steady.

"You're under starter's orders."

There was then a wait of between three and eight seconds (starter's prerogative) before the laggy was released and the riders all pedalled like madmen to the first bend, leaning into the tight corner with the inside leg providing balance.

Both my brothers had persuaded me to go and play "starter" for them in the intervening period (I'd do anything for a No 6 Tipped) and I became quite adept at it, especially when loads of their mates came along too.

The first match I remember was the Eagles versus Stradbroke Arrows, who had been around for a while and were rated as one of the top two teams (the other being the pretentiously named Sheffield Tigers) The guys rode mostly on self-built bikes, which had "Canadian Bends" handlebars, small cranks and cogs (32-18) no

Gee'or Ruwerin

gears or brakes, straight forks and gripster tyres. Forerunners of today's Mountain Bikes.

A meeting was based on conventional speedway with similar sized teams and the same scoring system (3-2-1-0) and the guy who got to the first bend first, was often the winner.

On that first day Stradbroke gave us a caning, but there was enough there to indicate potential, and sure enough as the season progressed, both Cross teams gave good accounts of themselves and finished above stalwarts like Park Wood Springs in the league.

The following season both our teams were a match for any of their rivals, and we hosted a few major meetings on our field, including the Yorkshire Championships, which was won by one of my brothers. He still has the Silver Sash to this day.

By the time I was old enough to join in the fun, the craze had dissipated and I never really got to ride, which was just as well really 'cause I was rubbish.

Chapter Nineteen

On The Town

On one occasion, when I was waggin' it on my own (Yew Lane must have had football that day) I decided to pop into town for a bit of excitement.

I got a 49 to Bridge Street, walked towards Lady's Bridge and turned up into the Castle Market. I wandered around for a bit, looking at the Harringtons in Harrington's, and the Ben Sherman's in Bunneys, before having a cup o'tea stood up while chatting to Alan Booth, whose red and white butchers apron was covered in offal and sheep's lights. The Meat and Fish Market was a real hive of activity. Boxes of veg were being carted along walkways, butchers shouted coarse remarks to each other, and the catering stalls were stacked to the rafters with old people chain smoking woodys. The strong smell of raw meat and fish assaulted my tender nostrils and followed me around for the rest of the day

In the Co-Op on Snig Hill, I got into the lift which was operated by a woman of about 96, who was sat on a three legged stool wearing a smock which may have fitted before the war, but hadn't since. If Henry Ford had made a Model-T lift, this was surely it. The inside walls were of highly varnished timber, arranged in vertical planks, with a large irrelevant mirror on the back wall. As the lift took off, the grinding of gears and cogs strained against Newton's fourth law to elevate me two floors. I was planning to get a new pair of Adidas Santiagos, but to my delight, the sports section was promoting the new Georgie Best boot, with side lacing and rotating studs. I walked around in a pair for about five minutes, repeatedly kicking an imaginary ball then jumping up to head it, before leaving a disappointed sales clerk behind and heading off down the world's biggest spiral staircase. I made a note of the film showing at The ABC, "They Shoot Horses Don't They?" (about a Dance Marathon? No thank you!) before getting dirty looks from a snotty cosmetics woman at the entrance to Cockayne's. My dad had just bought a gas stove coffee percolator from No 6 Coupons, and I wanted to see how much they were in a real shop. The models in Cockayne's were of a much higher spec, and would have required an iron lung's worth of tokens had they accepted this form of currency. They didn't. There was also a lovely China teapot with a matching cup and saucer, decorated with an amber flower motif and green leaves. I made a mental note to try and buy it my mum for Christmas, but that would depend on the residents of Rocher and Yew Greave being kind with their seasonal tips for the paper boy.

Next stop was Walsh's, another shop where we couldn't afford anything, but was always good for a gander. They had uniforms for my old school and I sneered as I caught site of the starlit Green 'N' Gold hanging above a curtained fitting room. It brought on a mild form of the Post Traumatics, and would do so today if it still existed. Their coffee percolators were a bit cheaper but still more than I would be willing to pay. I had tried to persuade dad to get a battery operated transistor radio, but he simply wouldn't listen. Tony Blackburn would have to remain a radiogram experience.

On the third or fourth floor of Walsh's was a small café which did a nice line in toasted tea-cakes. I was starting to feel a bit peckish so decided to invest my dinner money. I carried the tray over to a window seat, trying hard not to spill a drop of Ringtons, and plonked it down. The view was lovely. I could see up High Street towards Fargate, down Snig Hill to Peter Robinsons, and along Arundel to the Top Rank. At the junction below me, it seemed as though workmen had set out to dig the biggest hole ever! It stretched from Walsh's to Cockayne's to C&A to Fitzalan SQ. It was big enough for buses to fall into it, although I don't think any did. What on earth they could be digging for? A swimming pool maybe?

I caught a bus outside Walsh's, which went along Fargate, and turned left down Pinstone Street. "Paint Your Wagon" was showing at The Gaumont. A popular film because it featured Lee Marvin's "Wandering Star", but my sister said it was just "Seven Brides" with different songs. Ray Allen's Closing Down Sale was now in it's third year, and someone was building a giant egg box in the Peace Gardens. I got off at Suggs and, opposite Pauldens, walked around the corner to the best shop in Sheffield. Redgates!!

Redgates was a toy shop and then some. As well as stocking every toy known to man (I desperately wanted a Johnny Seven) they had interactive displays. There was a Meccano village with a Lego helicopter hovering above it, a train set with tunnels and hills and pylons, Action Men with a wide range of killing implements, and best of all, a Subbuteo Stadium with two teams, a Spion Kop, floodlights, and lots of other realistic accessories. One of the staff was playing against kids one at a time, up to the first goal. I got in line and after what seemed like a year, got my turn. I was England to his Brazil, and I quickly got into my stride, deft flicks demonstrating my aplomb. It wasn't long before I lifted the roof off the net when Franny Lee caught a half volley from just outside the area. After doing a lap of honour I had a go at juggling three highly coloured cloth balls - badly, did a "walking The Dog" with a Lunar 99, and had a stationary ride on a Raleigh Chopper.

Coming out into the sunlight, I had to blink to adjust my eyes. I'd been lost in toyland for much longer than I'd thought. Shops just didn't get any better than that. I still had a couple of hours more to kill, so reverted to that perennial favourite, playing the lifts in Cole Brothers. As I walked past Hornes on the corner of Barkers Pool, I saw that they were marketing their own "Ben Shermans". The mannequin wore a particularly nice, pale blue with maroon stripes, number, but being Hornes, I couldn't possibly afford it Truth be told I probably couldn't afford to even look in the window.

Once in Coles I was on familiar territory. This was where mum exercised her middle class pretensions, and I felt as though I (nearly) belonged. It was an old fashioned store, think of "Are You Being Served", but had a friendly atmosphere. Downstairs was men's clothes and kitchen stuff. There was a tall fridge like the one in the Dick Van Dyke Show, with two doors. I only realised years later that one half was a freezer. Their percolators were even dearer than the Cockayne's model, but looked classy. Coles too had their own Ben Sherman style shirts, with the "Jonelle" label. In theory I could've got one on mum's account but my better judgement prevailed, although I was more than a little tempted. They were also stocking, for the first time I believe, Levi Jeans. I began formulating a plan to get my mum into Coles and then "discover" the Levis! "I'll pay you back Mum, honest!!"

On the top floor was a wide range of home hi-fi, probably the best in town. Radiograms in the finest idigbo and mahogany, Japanese tape decks with vertical reels, and of course, the obligatory Dansette, although these were now on their last legs. I drooled over a delightful Roberts tranny in Barclays blue plastic, but had no delusions. On one wall was large bank of colour TVs, the first I had seen, but they showed only the test card, Rag Tag and Bobtail being doggedly monochromatic. One of the hi-fis had a glass case which showed the many valves, glowing their amplification smugly. It was truly beautiful and I committed then to one day owning one. It hasn't yet happened.

I shopped around for a while longer, but was now getting Parson Cross withdrawal symptoms, so I headed back to the safety and comfort of Bridge Street, where an 89 was waiting just for me. As if the day wasn't already good enough, it turned out that the conductor was Mick Flaherty, a good mate of my brother's, and he waived the toll, allowing me to pocket sevenpence. We shared a Park Drive and had a chat about how crap De La Salle was, Mick hated it even more than I did if that's possible, and I promised to pass a message on to Our Pete.

I stayed on the bus as far as Chaucer shops, to help kill the last 15 minutes, then met up with the Yew Lane crowd on their way home and started getting myself into a "hard day at school" mood as I sauntered down the jennell.

Chapter Twenty

Waggin' it

For my last year at school I moved to St Pete's, down next to Colley Park. My mum insists that it was by mutual consent between her and the school's hierarchy, but the word 'Expelled' was always hovering in the background.

I was glad to leave grammar. I had no inclination to study, it was just the totally wrong time of my life. There were so many other brilliant things to do, that there was no way I was gonna be shut up in my bedroom writing a thesis on ox-bow lakes, or conjugating the verb "Avoir" into Negative Interrogative. I wanted to play football, go to Youth Club, smoke Parkies, and the myriad other activities a healthy 14 year old living on The Cross could get up to. That, and my complete antipathy to the school's regime, the para-miltary wing of the catholic church, (or "De La Salle Brothers" to give 'em their proper title), meant an inevitable early bath.

St Pete's was a different ball game. It was like Butlins. They had no uniforms, no discernible homework, and the emphasis on religious teachings was negligible. The head teacher was an elderly guy who was rarely seen, which was as it should be.

Attendance was less than compulsory, and if I managed 50% during that whole term, I would be surprised. I used to meet up with my pals from Yew Lane School, and the world was our oyster on an almost daily basis. We would go up to Greno and build a tarzan swing. We'd go to Ecco Park and scrump apples from the neighbouring orchard. We'd go down town and have a "cup o' tea stood up" in the Castle Market. It was a wonderful year. It seemed to be sunny every day. There was even a school bobby (Truant Officer) whose job it was to try and round us all up and get us back to school, but he either wasn't very good or just didn't bother. We could spot his bright red Vauxhall Viva a mile off, and would hide behind any available cover.

The time I did spend at school was mostly wasted. Apart from playing for the football team I didn't make much of a contribution at all. There were however two significant exceptions to that

Firstly, I discovered my love of reading, which is still with me today.

Although I had declared my intention of leaving school at 15, I was placed in the upper stream, alongside those guys who were staying on to take their CSEs. One of the core books for study that year was George Orwell's "Animal Farm". I had no desire to read it, but one afternoon during a free period I began thumbing through it, out of sheer boredom I guess.

Within five pages I was hooked. I loved this sinister story about the hierarchy among the farm and how they kept changing the rules to trap each other. I didn't get the political significance at the time, but I did enjoy the intrigue. I couldn't put it down,and had it finished in just a few days. I followed this by reading "Robinson Crusoe" and "Of Mice and Men", and I thoroughly enjoyed both. I even rejoined

Gee'or Ruwerin

Margetson Library, for the first time since I was about seven, and took out books on a regular basis.

The second thing was that I found a teacher who was that rarest of things, an inspiration. He was the history teacher, Jim McNerney.

He was everything a teacher should be. He was loud, ebullient, confident and very, very funny. He was very knowledgeable, and could converse with equal enthusiasm on the subjects of Florence Nightingale or George Best. He was a natural orator, and when he spoke, kids listened.

It was from Jim that I learnt that it is better to be proficient in many subjects rather than an expert in just the few, a philosophy I have tried to continue into later life.

I was rarely absent on History days.

Towards the end of the school year, about May time, those of us who were leaving were visited by a Youth Employment Officer. Now, in them days, these guys had it easy. The big factories would soak up school leavers like a giant sponge and all the YE team had to do was to point them in the right direction.

My problem was that I didn't want to work in the factories, I wanted to be a telephone engineer.

"Aah, sit down Stephen. Now it says here that you want to be a telephone Engineer?"

Yes sir

"Have you considered a craft apprenticeship? The EITB (Engineering Industry Training Board) is now doing some wonderful courses, and you can train for a career in milling or turning."

No I don't want to go in't factries sir. I'm better wi' 'lectronics than wi mekkle.

"You could even take your CSE's as you train….."

But I don't like mekklework.

"…and go on to study at the City and Guilds. How does that sound?"

Can't I be a telephone engineer? GPO?

"Look" passing across two cards…

"I'll book you a couple of interviews. Here's one for John Bedfords, and one for

Tony (eldest brother - left) and Mick (youngest brother) in 1975

Brother Tony's 21st birthday

Gee'or Ruwerin

Easterbrook and Allcards. Let me know how you get on. Next!"

But sir I...

"Thank you Stephen, Next!"

Barry Hines got it spot on in 'Kes'.

I was offered both jobs (How? I tried my best not to get 'em!) and took the one at Bedfords.

And so it was that three weeks after my 15th birthday, I walked out of school for the last time and faced the long trek up Wordsworth. I guess it should have been a bit momentous but to be honest I'd had enough, and was ready to take on the world as a money earner. Looking back it seems that I was extremely young, but that didn't matter at the time. I was free from the shackles of education. Everything to do with school, English, Maths, Jogger and History, would now be...well, history!

Look out world, here comes Bushy!

Chapter Twenty One

Margetson Chip'oil

The best chip'oil on The Cross at that time was at Margetson.

It was also the most mysterious, as its opening hours were a closely guarded secret, known only to a discreet few.

It used to open only two or three times a week, and when word got out that the fat was simmering, the queue would quickly build up, going round the large interior tiled wall, then snaking out through the door, often reaching as far as the doctor's gate.

Little kids would run up'n'down Wordsworth shouting.

"Chippie's oppen!!"

Hoards of couples would stream out of Colley Club, carrying a pint of John Smiths and a rum'n'pep, their pie'n'peas going stale on the table.

"Wee-er are yore lot gooin'?"

"Chip'oil's open!"

Tombola games were abandoned in midstream. ("Eeeh, duz tha kno', I were sweatin' on twenny six for't four corners) Sometimes The Turn would come out to see why the audience was stood outside a chip shop? Bobby Knutt used to get a portion sent across to his dressing room, and always managed to get a plug in for his favourite chippy.

As well as sporadic opening hours, they also had a novel way of keeping the produce fresh.

Instead of having a steady trickle of fresh chips, they used to wait until they ran out, then Mrs Lee would shout "More Chips!!"

At this point, the ginger haired family who ran the place, would get the chipper out and begin the process of making some fresh. They brought it into the main shop so that spectators could marvel at its ingenuity (imagine Bessemer demonstrating his newly invented converter).

The tatties were ceremonially poured in at one end. The machine kicked into life, sounding a bit like a Francis Barnett, and minutes later, something resembling a pile of albino slugs would slowly emerge from the other end and drop into a yellow bucket, causing the line of customers to break into spontaneous applause. Eventually, enough of these were produced to justify dropping them into the sizzling fryer, kicking out enough steam to power a small train.

Of course, by this time the queue was nearly round to the Tavern, and kids were keeling over from starvation. The priest had to come over from Tommy More's and administer Extreme Unction to some of 'em.

Mind you, when the chips did eventually come, they were the best for miles around. They were that hot that I had to blow on 'em or they would burn my tongue. I shook the vinegar bottle over 'em for all it was worth, until the liquid ran out of the sides and up my arm. The visible vinegar fumes would drift slowly

Gee'or Ruwerin

upwards, as I sucked in through my nose, and took in a lungful of the delightful aroma. An indulgence which has followed me to this day.

Fish was a rarity, as it was so expensive, but at Margo chippy you would raid your piggy bank for a bob's worth o'cod. The batter was as crisp as it gets and the fish inside was quite delightful. They couldn't cook them fast enough, and were always waiting on the next batch.

"Anybody not want fish?"

"Yeah, can I just have fish-cake and chips Mrs Lee?"

I don't think that there is a chippy in Sheffield today producing such nice cod in batter, except maybe Brenda's on Earl Way (next to Violet May's)

The Ritz in its later bingo hall guise

Chapter Twenty Two

Youth Clubs

During my early working life, before I could afford to go the pub each evening, I was an enthusiastic member of the Youth Clubs which dotted the area.

Living in the epicentre of The Cross, close to the junction of Wordsworth and Deerlands, I had easy access to Mansell, Meynell and Colley YCs. All fine institutions in their own right,

In the late '60s and into the early '70s, I could go to a club each weekday evening, and often did, meeting many of the same people at all three.

My favourite, and the one at which I felt most at home, was Mansell. Each Monday, Wednesday and Friday, myself, and the crew of guys who were my best mates, would go up for a game of table tennis or darts, and maybe even a go on the pinball.

"Oi, Wriggo. Ar tha gunna't club?"

"Cooerse I am. Is Deso gooin?"

"Aah 'e is. E's comin strayt from't bus"

"Is e on afters?"

"Nayew. E's doing a dubble cuss er a big order"

There was a disco, consisting basically of a square room with bench seats and tables down one side. The walls were painted black and the fluorescent strip lighting was ultra-violet. This paid dividends whenever a girl came in wearing a dark top with a white bra, as the bra shone bright purple through the top and was the focus of every boy's eye. It also had (didn't they all?) a mirror-ball, which spun frenetically in time to the heavy beat of the ultra loud music. You couldn't hear yourself smoke but boy it was great fun. Occasionally they would play a medley of WW2 singalong songs ("My old man said follow the van" that kind of thing) and we would all sing our hearts out – inserting a few dirty lyrics whenever we could. Then it was back to Creedence or Blood Sweat and Tears.

"Put Chirpy Chirpy Cheep Cheep on!"

"Tha muss bi jokin'. It's Band o' Gold next."

It was a great place for boys and girls to mix in comparative safety. I met my first girlfriend at the club. A gorgeous kid from Buchanan who was a big part of my life for some three years, on and off, and I know of at least one couple, still living on The Cross, who met aged 14 at Mansell Club. They've now been married well over 30 years. (Jeez!)

The team who ran the club (Len, Jackie and others) were all in their thirties and were really dedicated people. I know they got paid but it wasn't a huge amount, and they did often go beyond the call of duty, training the football team and running guys to and from games. This despite being on the receiving end of constant witty banter from the scruffy kids.

Gee'or Ruwerin

"Nah then Len, wiv ad a fone call from't 1950s. Thi want ther drainpipes back."

"Jackie. Are yer sellin' them puppies?"

There was a bit of fighting, especially when the Foxhill kids came looking for a ruckus, but generally it provided a much needed sanctuary from factory life and all that that brought with it.

The Saturday Youth Clubs League saw some very passionate football, and the rivalry between the three local clubs was intense. Losing to Colley meant a long walk home along Remington, and when Mansell won the league one year, we celebrated in style with a disco party at the club. We even got Pete Howe's band to come and play a session for us. (Hit me over the heeaad….with a fire extinguisherrr!!)

I was mediocre at best, but they'd forgotten to tell me, so I turned out week after week, scoring lots of goals because I'd never learnt how to miss.

"Duz tha kno' Bushy, if't ball bounced off thy arse it'd goo in't goil."

I remember one memorable home game against Meynell. I'd gone back to bed after an early morning shift at Millspaugh, and was woken up at three that afternoon by Len bashing on our front door and my mam shouting upstairs. Five minutes later I ran onto the pitch, still eating a slice of toast, and scored two goals in a 5-3 win.

"Thy ought ter bring thi too-erst evry week Bushy, it meks thi play berrer."

" Ah Kno'. Neks week am avin a T boo-ern steakl!"

I do sometimes feel that in an age where knives, guns and drugs play a large part in adolescent society, and many people fear seeing gangs of kids congregating on street corners, we've done our kids a disservice by letting the Youth Club system elapse. While much less than perfect, it was a great way to supervise kids and yet allow them to let off steam in a controlled environment.

Any chance they'll come back?

Chapter Twenty Three

Pubs

As we got a little older, and sprinted headlong into an early adulthood, Youth Clubs started to lose their attraction and were slowly being elbowed to one side in favour of pubs.

As with YCs, I lived bang in the middle of three – four if you counted Colley Club (nobody did) – all within five minutes walk of our house. They each had their charms but were quite different in the fare they offered.

The Parson Cross Hotel, on Deerlands Avenue and Buchanan Crescent, close to the Wordsworth-Deerlands junction and the 17 bus stop, was a big sprawling building which had probably at one point been an actual hotel. It had a whole host of upstairs function rooms, many of which were never used, a large downstairs function room to the rear, last seen on Bungi's wedding day, and two main drinking rooms at the front, the Tap Room and the Lounge (or best room). There was a single doorway entrance from Deerlands, and you turned left into the lounge, or right into the tap. If you turned right though, you had to be very careful.

Now, it's easy to be critical, and heaven knows that when it comes to design I'm at the very back of the skills queue, but even I wouldn't put a dartboard just inside the entrance, in such a way that if you opened the door and stepped quickly in, double top could develop a whole new meaning, especially if Lambchops was throwing. The trajectory of the darts passed directly across the path of the newcomer – and once or twice a year someone would get spiked. I always crawled in on my hands and knees just to be sure.

It was a nice pub though, always a pleasant atmosphere. The décor was very basic. In the Tap Room it was a sort of dull brown, with simple wooden chairs and tables and a lino floor. They kept it fairly clean, but these were the days when a man would get off the 17 bus, or indeed the 194, and nip in for a quencher before going home. Often they would be dressed in a boiler suit, steel capped boots (Cappers) and the ubiquitous donkey jacket. Work in the rolling mills and drop forges was often dirty, and few companies had decent showers, so if you popped in The Cross before eight o'clock on a midweek evening, there would always be a few punters with panda faces, stood at the bar chatting about the day's cogging back or hooking up.

Some nights we would sneak into the lounge where Deso's dad, or maybe Trevor Kirby, would be banging out the old standards on the upright which hid in the corner. "There's an old mill by the stream" "Old Bull and Bush" that kinda thing. This was a bit plusher with faux leather padding on the bench seats, clean beer mats, and of course, a carpet. Working clothes were forbidden here. The lounge didn't start filling up until after nine o'clock, and most men wore trousers and a shirt, with a jacket and tie at weekends – and their wives and girl friends usually dressed up a little too. It was always sign of being in a serious relationship if you took your girlfriend in the lounge.

They served a very passable Whitbread Trophy, a slightly less passable Whitbread

Gee'or Ruwerin

Tankard, and weren't too keen on establishing proof of age – just proof of payment, so it was very popular with those who weren't quite 18 yet, and I continued to be a regular customer up until the point when I left home.

When I was at primary school, the Wordsworth Tavern had a been a small, pale grey, flat-roof building, square on to the street and facing down Colley Rd. I never went inside but can remember standing out front Penny-for-the-guy-ing. Even in those early days, none of the money went on fireworks. Smiths Crisps, with the blue salt twisty, Dandelion and Burdock (see who can do the loudest burp!), and of course, 5 Parkys – but never fireworks.

During the late sixties it was demolished and replaced with a fancy new purpose built modern pub, katy cornered onto the main road and Margetson Crescent, with a decent size car park. I didn't go in the Tav too often, as one of my elder brothers was a barman there and I didn't want to cramp his style, but have fond memories of my few visits. It had a decent jukebox, and if you went in the early evening, before the crush started, they would turn it up nice and loud for you. The Isley Brothers' version of "I Hear A Symphony" was usually my first choice, followed by Paul Simon's "Paranoia Blues" and "Does Anybody Really Know What Time It Is" by Chicago.

Another key event was when there was a decent act on at The Club (Colley WMC). We would walk across in a mob from the tavern, carrying our pints, sit through a session of Bitter Suite or Charlie Williams, and then carry a fresh pint back to the tavern.

In between turns, the club would have a few games of Tombola. This was a sacred ritual, and if silence wasn't observed during the call out of the numbers, then you could be stoned to death or even hung drawn and quartered. Being noisy by nature it was easier for us to go back across the road and wait for the second coming.

At the end of the bingo, you would write your name on the back of your ticket and these were then collected, placed in a drum, and a winner pulled out. They usually asked someone sat at the front to do the draw.

One evening, we had occupied a front table. Jinks was asked to pull out a winner. He still had his own ticket tucked in his hand, which he dipped in the drum , rolled around a bit, then pulled out and shouted "The Winner is..."

Of the three local pubs, my favourite by quite some distance was The Beagle.

I first went in on my way home from Mansell Youth Club aged about 16 and a half. The landlord was an old (well he seemed old to us) Jewish guy called Joe Williams. He and his wife ran a lovely establishment. Everything from the cleanliness to the friendly staff was of a standard which I've seldom seen equalled in the years since. The beer was Joshua Tetleys best cask bitter, which ironically, is now eagerly sought by Real Ale guys with pony tails and ill fitting shorts who hold it up to the light and comment on its "Opaque Capacity" and "Spasmodic Density". JUST DRINK IT!!

The fixtures and fittings were principally of a rich red colour, and seemingly every available accessory, beer mats, pump towels, ash trays, was decorated with the smiling face of the monocled huntsman himself. Joe was a proper landlord, and took a great deal of pride in the quality of his draught, making sure it was always up to scratch

Gee'or Ruwerin

There was a lovely mix of drinkers, which included a few local women who came on their own, their husbands doing a night shift at George Clarke's or driving a Mushet truck over to Holland. There never seemed to be any stigma attached, even to a couple of widows who were regulars. Most of the guys who came back night after night, were steelworkers of various calibre, and shift work played a big part in peoples lives. One or two were brickies on Gleeson's rapid expansion programme, where any unused land could be built on, and there was a local window cleaner who was never too far from a pint.

Here I learned to play, and became quite good at darts. The boards were a bit different from those used today, in that they had no trebles and no 25 (outer bullseye). Rather than play games which involved totting up high scores, ours were of the "Round-the-board-on-the-doubles" kind. Three arrers at double-one. If you hit it, three at double-two etc. There was also an few fun games based loosely on Snooker, Poker and Knock-out whist, but the rules have faded from the memory. Our best player of that era was a miner called Bernard who, in his fifties, started a coughing fit while going for double-six, went outside for some fresh air, and died from pneumoconiosis sat on the perimeter wall. I always avoided double-six after that.

There was also a lot of card playing, but that wasn't my bag. I found out very early that if you were rubbish at three card brag, and I was the epitome of rubbishness, you could easily lose a lot of money. It wasn't unusual to see someone come straight from work on a Thursday and then have to take an empty pay packet home to the wife.

We had dominoes too, fives and threes, which was scored using a crib board. There was a bit of money changing hands here but it was shrapnel rather than silver, and on a really bad night you still only lost five bob max.

The wide array of characters who came through door, always ensured an interesting time.

There was Pete Howe, the closest Parson Cross came to producing a John Lennon. Although not academically endowed, he taught himself to play a very mean guitar, and his band toured the local pubs and clubs before Pete slid into a Syd Barratt-like cloistered retirement in his mid 20s. I can still sing all the words to "King of the Saucepans" and "Loves to love the loved".

Deso, a friend of mine since junior school days, had developed into a very quirky teenager and had his sights set in becoming a recluse by the time he was 30.

Others too numerous to mention gave my adolescence a vivid backdrop, and I'm eternally grateful to them all.

I was in The Beagle the night Britain went decimal – 15 Feb 1971 – and was amused at the chaos involved when, on purchasing a pint of Joshua's finest, instead of getting a threepenny-bit for change from their half-crowns, Joe handed them one and a half new P. There was certainly a few choice words exchanged that night, and Ted Heath's heritage was called into question a number of times.

(Reprise)

On my fortieth birthday, having travelled the world in pursuit of the King's Shilling, I contacted a lot of old friends and one Saturday night about 55 people met up in the Beagle. The landlord at that time, himself one of my childhood chums, laid on a

Gee'or Ruwerin

lovely spread, salmon sarnies and celery dips, and although the pub had changed in structure, I was thrilled that the atmosphere hadn't, and we ended up celebrating, not just my birthday, but being born and raised on The Cross.

We were very fortunate indeed.

Parson Cross view

Chapter Twenty Four

The Epilogue - Childhood's end

In his lovely poem "The Road Not Taken" Robert Frost talks about those times in life when you hit a metaphorical fork in the road. The decision, do I go left, do I go right? The answer may very well define the rest of your life.

This can apply to all those big moments: Shall I get married, shall I not? Should I buy a house in Ecclesfield or wait until I can afford one at Grenoside? Do I stop smoking now or will I just have one more lovely Park Drive?

In each case the decision made can be life affecting, and it is sensible to weigh up all the odds before proceeding.

There are also times when small decisions can be equally dramatic, but you're not aware of this at the time. Do we shop at Margetson or Buchanan? Should I drink in The Parson Cross Hotel or The Wordsworth Tavern?

And in my case, which bus do I catch? The 49 or the 53?

Frost also says that, whatever your decision, you can never know how things would have turned out if you had chosen the other way. You can maybe make a few intelligent guesses, but you'll never know for sure.

If I had caught the 49 that Tuesday morning in April, 1976, I no doubt would have gotten off at Bridge Street, and walked up Snig Hill into town. I may well have popped into a few employment agencies, there was one in Fitzalan Square I had in mind, and had a look at what was available. It's possible that I would have gone down to Castle Market, going in at the corner entrance next to Harrington's, and had a "cup o'tea stood up" at Sally's. I was after a new pair of Levi's so a quick visit to Bunney's was on the cards.

But I didn't get on the 49, Frost's "Road Not Taken"

I caught the 53.

At the beginning of that long hot summer, the hottest and longest in living memory, I was at a bit of a loose end.

I'd had a couple of steady girlfriends, and a handful of not so steady ones, but these relationships had petered out and I was currently between engagements. Many of my friends were settling down, and the pipe and slippers brigade seemed to be increasing membership exponentially. Even The Beagle, that beacon of consistency in an ever changing world, was starting to feel alien. Joe, the landlord, had moved on, the top darts player, Bernard, had died suddenly (he actually died in the pub, playing darts!!) and the new manager had decorated the place. They'd even put a carpet down for heaven's sake. What's that all about?

My older brothers and sisters had all left home – twice in some cases – and Mum was on her own, Dad having run off with the girl from the Stamps counter at the GPO in town.

I had been working for over five years, and had experienced a number of different jobs during that time. I'd started before leaving school, by cleaning windows on

Gee'or Ruwerin

The Cross – Donovan Rd and parts of Wordsworth - for beer money. This required me to wag it two days a week – no problem!!

As for proper jobs, I'd done some engineering, some labouring, and had drifted into administration. Although I was proud to say that I'd never been out of work, I didn't really know what

Colley Working Mens Club

I wanted to be when I grew up. I was presently working in a heavy engineering plant which is now buried under Meadowhall Car Park. (I reckon the Supertram runs through my old office!!) I'd been there for nearly two years, working long days tallying the hours that welders and platers booked to various projects, and making sure that bonus payments were accurate (they never were).

Because of the North Sea Oil Industry, the large storage vessels being manufactured here were in big demand, as they were destined for the sea bed off the coast of Aberdeen, where they would store the crude being sucked out of the ocean. They were really massive – often as long as 120 ft, and some 20 ft in diameter, and my biggest memory is of seeing them being police escorted up to the M1 and heading off towards Leeds and beyond.

The job demanded seven day working, and lots of midweek overtime. The pay was really good – we were some of the first hundred quid a week workers – but it was really knackering. Especially as I was burning the candle at both ends and even, some weeks, in the middle as well. It wasn't easy getting up at 6:30 on a Sunday morning when I'd been dancing the night away at Tiffany's until well after two.

Inevitably, this all caught up with me and I started having days off, and eventually, one Monday morning, the boss called me in and read me my tea leaves.

"You know the score Steve" he was a friendly guy.

"If you don't want to work seven days, there's a big queue of guys who will be happy to jump in"

I assured him that I would be more diligent and apply myself to the task.

"OK that's good" happier now.

"and next time you don't come in..." this sounded ominous "you might as well pop down the Labour Exchange and start hunting."

I was suitably warned.

That evening, I went to The Beagle, planning to have a couple of quick pints, and get an early night. It was a warm evening and some of my pals were sat outside when I got there. One of my childhood friends was celebrating his 21st, so the Tetleys was flowing freely and it would have been rude not to join in. Someone took orders for The Lotus on Chaucer Rd, so by about nine I was well into the ale, and chomping through a Chinese Prawn Curry. The birthday guy, Pete, felt obliged to get a round of shorts in, so I indulged in a Southern Comfort or two. When we got kicked out, it was late o'clock, and I staggered along Knutton with a couple of mates, and headed down the jennel to glorious sleep.

Gee'or Ruwerin

I still don't know to this day if I set my alarm or not, but it was well past 9am when I woke up - already two hours late.

I resigned myself to the inevitable, and went back to sleep.

I eventually crawled out of bed at midday, and had a bath and a bowl of Puffa Puffa Rice before deciding to go out looking for a new job. I was already wondering what kind of thing to aim for. Although I was considered intelligent, I had no certificates from school, and even my further education courses had all seemed to fizzle out before I could get any qualifications. A 16 year old could always learn on the job, but at the age of 20 you were expected to bring a few skills to the table.

I put some clean clothes on, walked up past the Alan Pond and headed for a bus. There was a 53 at the terminus, and I thought about crossing the road for the 49 like I normally would, as it usually came a few minutes before the 53 pulled out, but I was feeling so sorry for myself that I just got on, paid the driver, and sat at the back staring at the future.

A full ten minutes after the 49 had come and gone, my bus pulled out and chugged slowly up Deerlands on its routine journey to town. All the way I was playing various scenarios through my head, toying with a number of ideas, none of which were very inspiring. At Mowbray Street, the bus stopped outside the offices of John Bedford, my very first employer, and I stared in through the window, imagining myself back in there. This happened again on Nursery Street with the Sheffield Testing Works, and I degenerated from "feeling sorry for myself" down into a positive sulk.

As we pulled around the corner at the Bull and Mouth I got up and rang the bell. The bus pulled into the stop at Castlegate and I stepped off into the bright sunshine.

As I stopped and looked around for ideas, I noticed a poster in the window of the Armed Forces Recruiting Office. It showed a smartly dressed young man, wearing an army green shirt and trousers and a brown button-smock with two shiny chevrons on the upper arm He was stood by a workbench, and in front of him was big valve radio, opened for investigation. A couple of valves lay on their side beside the unit. He had a soldering iron in one hand, and a length of solder in the other and was getting stuck in.

The slogan on the poster read "Join The Royal Signals…"

Then lower down "…and train to be a Radio Technician"

Without thinking, I pushed open the door and walked in

"Hi" said a highly polished sergeant in dress uniform, "can I help you?"

"Yes" I answered.

"I'd like to join The Royal Signals and train to be a Radio Technician."

About the **Author**

Steve Bush was born Stephen Paul Bush, in June 1955. He was the seventh of Sydney and Angela Bush's eight children and born in the front bedroom of 387, Wordsworth Avenue, in the very heart of Parson Cross

He attended St Thomas More Primary School in Grenoside, where he was a member of both the football and rounders teams, until the age of 11. After passing the 11-Plus, he moved on to De La Salle Grammar at Burngreave. At the age of 14, at the special request of the head teacher, he transferred to St Peter's Comprehensive School at Parson Cross.

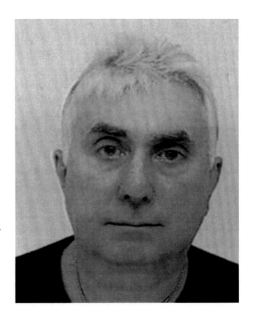

After leaving school at 15, without the burden of qualifications, he worked in various factories and foundries, usually as a labourer and occasionally in administration.

At the age of 20, as a short term stop-gap, he joined The Royal Corps of Signals as a Radio Engineer.

Twenty years later, as Staff Sergeant Bush, and having seen active service in Northern Ireland, Central America and the first Gulf War, he returned to Sheffield with his wife and two daughters, where he has lived ever since

Since leaving the army, Steve has worked in telecommunications, and is currently part of the research and development team at a large Finnish telecoms company. He recently celebrated his 33rd wedding anniversary and will become a granddad for the third time in May of this year

Steve's main hobbies are reading Swedish crime fiction, watching European and Japanese films, and telling his grand children stories about growing up on Parson Cross.

Gee'or Ruwerin

Parson Cross view